STAMPING
OUR
HISTORY

STAMPING
OUR
HISTORY

The Story of the United States Portrayed on Its Postage Stamps

By
Charles Davidson and
Lincoln Diamant

A Lyle Stuart Book

Published by
Carol Publishing Group

New York

Editorial Offices
600 Madison Avenue, New York NY 10022

Sales and Distribution Office
120 Enterprise Avenue South, Secaucus NJ 07094

Distributed in Canada by The Musson Book Company
Division of General Publishing Company, Ltd., Don Mills, Ont.

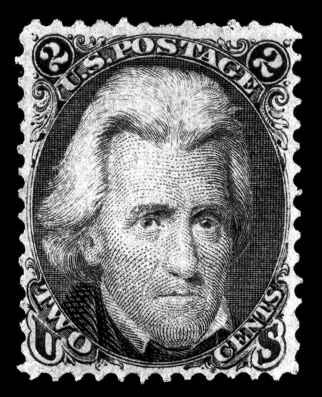

Library of Congress Cataloging-in-Publication Data

Davidson, Charles.
Stamping our history: the story of the United States portrayed on its postage stamps /
by Charles Davidson and Lincoln Diamant.
p. cm. "A Lyle Stuart book ."
Includes philatelic reference section, index.
ISBN 0-8184-0532-5 : $49.95
1. Postage-stamps--Topics--United States.   2. Postage-stamps--United States--History.
3. United States--History--Miscellanea.
I. Diamant, Lincoln.   II. Title.
HE6183.U54D38   1990
769.56'49973--dc20
90-38791 CIP

Manufactured in the United States of America
First Edition

*For our parents---who opened our eyes
to stamp collecting, and our minds to history*

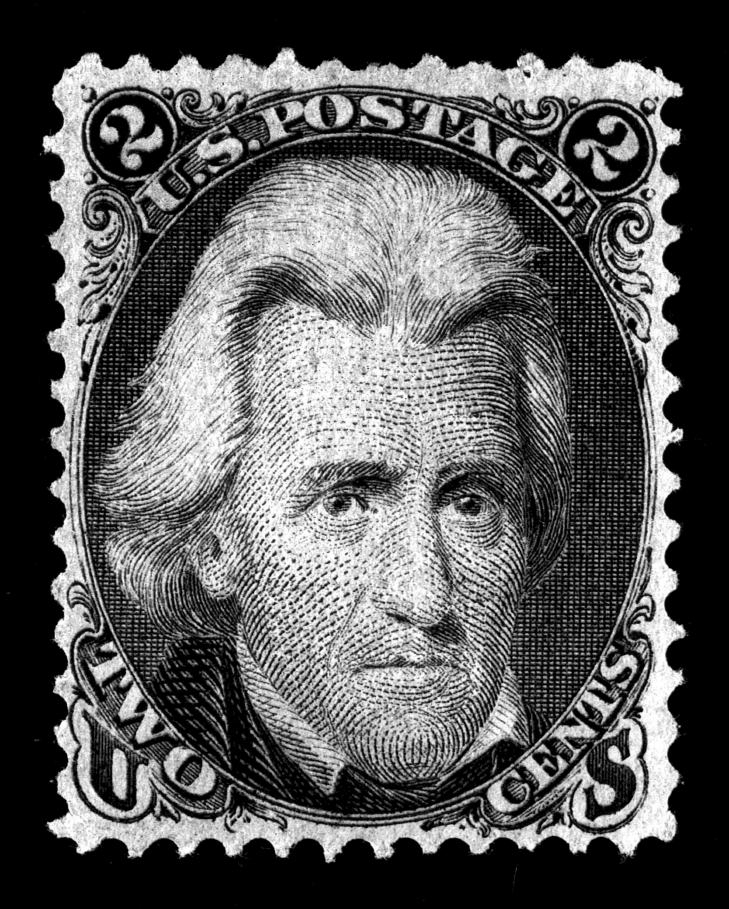

PREFACE

A"*Multum In Parvo*"---much in little.

ll the graphic images in this book are derived from nearly a century and a half of United States postage stamps. Most of these Lilliputian designs are less than two inches square. Don't be misled by such modest proportions; what they lacked in size they have made up for in content and quantity. Since 1847, billions of these colorful miniatures have come from the presses, keeping our postal system afloat---and celebrating important individuals and major events in the history of our country.

Rich detail created by skilled engravers has allowed most of these stamps to serve as strong statements of our national artistic expression. *Stamping Our History* greatly enlarges the historic imagery---in some instances over 2000%---allowing you to "see into" surprising nooks and crannies of these postal gems.

The stamps in this book were selected for their intrinsic beauty as well as visual information. Where certain subjects were repeated over the years, the authors have usually chosen the older examples---"stepped up" from the initial delicate engraving onto steel plates, one stamp at a time, using a three-stage process called "transfer rolling." With the exception of an early experiment in offset printing at the end of World War I, United States stamps until 1965 were produced by steel engraving.

Many of today's multicolored special issues, created in the explosion of sophisticated and complex printing techniques, are little more than tiny magazine illustrations. For both image and subject matter, the authors would prefer not to lick stamps such as "*Savings and Loans,*" "*Take a Bite Out of Crime,*" or "*Alcoholism... You can beat it!*" for our own mailing envelopes--- although a century hence those bits of glued paper may mature into some form of socio-historical commentary.

Until then, choosing mainly from the first hundred years of traditional United States postal designs, *Stamping Our History* vividly illustrates our useable past in magnificent detail. This unique word-and-picture celebration of our country can be handed down with delight from generation to generation.

CONTENTS

INTRODUCTION

Credit goes to the British.

In 1837, to cope with mushrooming postal volume, a man named Rowland Hill (later Sir Rowland) introduced three logical "Post Office Reforms." The new rules turned upside down the centuries-old English procedures for mailing a letter:

- ❦ Mail could now go *anywhere* in the British Isles at the same rate---a penny a half-ounce.
- ❦ Postage was now paid by the *sender*---not the *addressee*.

And most important to the reader of this book:

- ❦ Payment was henceforth receipted by "*a bit of coloured paper, covered at the back by a glutinous wash, attached by the sender to the letter by applying a bit of moisture.*"

It took the United States almost a decade to really catch up with Sir Rowland.

Not until 1847 did the first official sheets of our own home-grown postage stamps come off a private engraver's press. American letter writers no longer had to depend on their local postmaster's signature on the envelope, or his inked "*PAID ALL*" crudely whittled from a bottle cork. The government permanently swept away such improvisations, with its new 200-stamp engraved sheets that portrayed the heads of two of America's greatest heroes---Benjamin Franklin and George Washington (#948).

Like the earliest stamps of countries all over the world, those first U.S. sheets were "imperforate"; you simply scissored off a stamp when you needed it. Ten years later came the more convenient tear-apart sheets, whose perforations have been with us ever since. (Each year, more than 75 tons of those minuscule punched-out wastepaper dots---called "chad"---fuel a special boiler at the Treasury Department's Bureau of Engraving and Printing.)

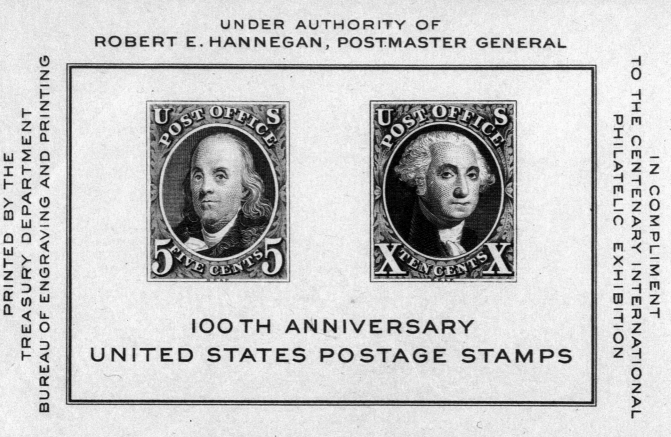

UNDER AUTHORITY OF
ROBERT E. HANNEGAN, POSTMASTER GENERAL

PRINTED BY THE
TREASURY DEPARTMENT
BUREAU OF ENGRAVING AND PRINTING

IN COMPLIMENT
TO THE CENTENARY INTERNATIONAL
PHILATELIC EXHIBITION

100TH ANNIVERSARY
UNITED STATES POSTAGE STAMPS

NEW YORK, N.Y., MAY 17-25, 1947

Postal graphics during our first two decades of stamp design continued with enscrolled busts of Franklin and Washington--- and occasionally Jefferson, Jackson, and Lincoln. Finally, in 1869, the government's printing contractor, the National Bank Note Company, took a creative plunge. To the heads of those presidents (and Franklin, our first Postmaster General), the company designers added some delicately engraved early American iconography: *Columbus Landing on San Salvador*, the *Declaration of Independence*, a pair of bald eagles, a Pony Express rider, the *S.S. Adriatic*, and a Baldwin locomotive.

Those seven stamps were still "definitive," or regular issues. "*Commemoratives*," those dramatically different special subjects in varying denominations, honoring recently-deceased personages or national events, were not invented until 1888 (by the Australian colony of New South Wales). But thanks to that initial inspiration of the National Bank Note engravers, all our little pay-as-you-go United States postal receipts immediately became something much grander---and far more collectible.

The mania for stamp collection had begun long before the issuance of commemoratives. As early as 1841, a young lady advertised in the London *Times* for "*generous and good-natured persons to assist her in collecting canceled postage stamps.*" Why did she want them? To add decoration to the walls of her dressing room.

Punch was quick to mock "such industriously idle people, as indefatigable in their efforts to collect Queens' heads as Harry the Eighth was to get rid of them." But the innocent contagion soon spread internationally.

In 1865, to denote the new aficionados of those tiny, colorful, easily available, and interesting pieces of paper, Georges Herpin coined the word "*philatelist*" to replace the original (and somewhat unnerving) "*timbromaniac.*" Greek roots were tortuously bent by M. Herpin to convey the "love of something untaxed," *i.e.*, the collection of already-paid-for postal receipts. Surprisingly, Herpin's word caught on. Despite a mocking *Punch*, saving stamps quickly found a permanent place among the world's great hobbies, with a slowly-growing preference for the unused object---much as a numismatist prizes the uncirculated in preference to the shopworn coin.

Acknowledging a growing worldwide fascination with such tiny postal tableaux, the first true United States commemoratives came from the engraver's press in 1893. That series celebrated both the 400th anniversary of the landing of Columbus, and the great Chicago World's Columbian Exposition. Century-old *"Columbians"* can still be found on dusty attic letters and packages. They can bring from six cents to thirteen hundred dollars, depending on denomination and condition.

Since the 1890's, when U.S. stamps first began to celebrate our country's history in an organized manner, commemorative postage has flowed from the presses in ever-increasing volume. The *"Columbians"* established a graphic postal pattern that continues today, with colorful tiny paper celebrations of great men and women and momentous historical events.

Unlike monarchies (constitutional and otherwise) where portraits (or silhouettes) of royalty tend to dominate a country's stamps, popular subjects from every era of American history are available to U.S. commemorative stamp designers. Stamps today also reflect the steady development and growth of American printing technology. From delicate transfer-rolled and sheet-printed steel engravings, later supplanted by one- and two-color rotary-printed designs, stamps now mirror the output of modern six- and eight-color gravure/intaglio presses.

During the early years of World War I, American industrial dependence on German-made aniline dyes was so great that a special shipment of various colored stamp ink dyes consigned to the Bureau of Engraving and Printing was actually carried by the U-boat *Deutschland* across the North Atlantic through a tight British blockade. The submarine discreetly deposited its precious cargo behind a hastily constructed high wooden fence on a Baltimore pier. Press photographers, naturally, were barred.

From the initial sketch to the finished mucilage-backed postage label, our stamps have captured current American aesthetics. Until recently, a handful of essentially anonymous postal designers exerted a subtle but enormous influence on America's everyday graphic taste. In the quarter century ending in 1957, four men---Victor S. McCloskey, Jr., Charles R. Chickering, William A. Roach, and William K. Schrage--- designed 83% of all United States postage stamps.

Fine art has always played a major role in stamp design:

- Subjects have ranged from copies of classic Gilbert Stuart paintings to colorful concoctions by the latest trendy American artists.
- A half century ago, during the 200th birthday celebration for our first president, the Post Office Department reproduced a full dozen Washington portraits---by seven different painters and sculptors, including Stuart, Peale, Trumbull, and Houdon. They are all in this book.
- In addition to works by Hokusai, Ter Borch, Memling, Lotto, Perugino, Moroni, Carracci, van Eyck, Ghirlandaio, Giorgione, Botticelli, Tiepolo, Cranach, Raphael, Lippi, Della Robbia, Chardin, Gainsborough, Goya, West, Copley, David, Audubon, Homer, Currier & Ives, Harnett, Eakins, Remington, Russell, Peto, Whistler, Cassatt, French, Borglum, Sloan, Benton, Grandma Moses, Indiana, Albers, Max, and Singer, many other paintings and designs by old masters and contemporary fine artists grace United States stamps, helping to turn such philatelic specialties into miniature "museum pieces."

Most of our art-oriented stamps are commemoratives, but commemoratives represent only one part of our colorful postal heritage. Airmail, revenue, regular issue, official, special delivery, even *postage due* receipts are among the billions of stamps that have come from private and government presses for 13 decades.

To the trail-blazing 1869 *Landing of Columbus* and *Declaration of Independence* have now been added hundreds of other graphic, historical, and artistic themes. Stamps in this book sample the great epochs of America: the land and its original inhabitants; the era of colonial discovery; the glorious Revolutionary years with patriot heroes and battlefields; the struggles of the new nation and its western expansion; the Civil War to preserve the federal union; the age of invention and industrial development; our participation in two world wars; and most recently, our daring ventures into space. One must admit the United States has always been a remarkable part of the world in which to live.

Whether you are fascinated by postage, history, art, or all three, this selection of our country's historic stamps will allow you to trace the destiny of North America from its earliest aboriginal times to the present. Unlike any other illustrations, these colorful bits of glued paper capture a special feeling of America. To see them "larger than life" offers striking new insights into our historic symbolism, the individuals it enshrines, and the nation it celebrates.

THE LAND

#746

Before all else, there was The Land.

The earliest explorers brought back unbelievable stories: besides a goodly assortment of rocks and rills, woods and templed hills, this part of the New World contained some astonishing "works of nature." But it took the opening of our West for Americans to truly appreciate the magnificent splendor of the United States wilderness.

Here was the land unchanged, much as it existed before the very first footprint of man. Here were spacious, primitive areas with such outstanding scenery and natural wonders that some form of preservation, for the benefit and inspiration of all, soon became a matter of national concern.

In 1872, triggered by the discovery of Yellowstone (#744), Congress surprised itself with a great idea: such magnificent pieces of U.S. real estate should be permanently set apart---inviolate---from private development and exploitation. Instead, they should become *a pleasure ground for the enjoyment of all the people.*"

That was a brand-new "made in America" concept of recreational land use, soon to spread through the civilized world.

From that sensible breakthrough came our National Park system, established within the U.S. Department of Interior. Its simple mandate, provided by Congress, was *"to conserve the scenery and natural and historic objects, in such manner and by such means as will leave them unimpaired for the enjoyment of future generations."*

May we never forget that weighty responsibility to "future generations," as we recall this glorious 1934 stamp series celebrating the creation of ten of our greatest national parks, stretching from Maine to California---from Montana to North Carolina (#745-748).

Surely every visitor has a favorite park in the system. High on the list must be Yosemite, established in 1890 in an incredible niche of the Sierras. Thanks in part to this lovely stamp, the mile-high granite bulk of El Capitan (#740) that looms above the valley entrance has become the perfect symbol of "the people's land"---a park system that now contains more than 13 million acres.

May it be preserved and enlarged forever.

U.S. PO

6¢

CRAT

How old is the American landscape? The immense stretches of geologic time are not that hard to comprehend.

Create your own "*time-line*" by visualizing a postage stamp ---like *#747*---lying flat atop a dime. Then, in your mind's eye, place the coin and stamp anywhere on top of the spectacular Great White Throne, in Utah's Zion National Park.

Assume this 2,394-foot-high peak to represent all the years of the Cenozoic Era---in ascending order, the Paleocene, Eocene, Oligocene, Miocene, and Pliocene Periods, beginning 65, 53, 37, 26, and 12 million years ago. Those were the geologic periods in which the raw materials of today's magnificently striated Zion landscape were laid down as sedimentary layers at the bottom of shallow southwestern seas---sands, muds, and calcium deposits that were slowly compressed into sandstones, shales, and limestones.

Gradually over tens of millions of years, those former underwater layers were raised thousands of feet by ever-changing shifts in the earth's surface. Exposed and sculpted by wind and rain, they now form the cliff walls of the Great White Throne--- and all the other brilliantly colored formations and deep canyons of Zion Park.

Now, consider the thickness of the *dime* and *stamp*.

The bottom of the dime represents that moment in time, about 12,000 years ago, when the first humans traversed the Bering isthmus into the New World. Slowly, generation after generation, they worked their way south, establishing different native American cultures---like the Utes, who would one day give their name to our 45th state.

The top of the dime (and the bottom of the stamp) reflects that moment in 1776 when Fathers Silvestre Vélez de Escalante and Francisco Dominguez became the first white men to travel westward from Santa Fe, to see what was going down in Utah. Finally, the thickness of the paper in *#747* represents our own era---the time of other white explorers; the Mormon settlers who christened "Zion"; and today's National Park visitors.

The ink on the stamp? After such a quick trip through 100 million years of an old country, the thickness of the ink can stand for the decade in which you sit reading this page---give or take an ink molecule or two.

When the ice dam of the North American continental glacier finally melted back into Canada 12,000 years ago, water from the Great Lakes could once again flow north over the Niagara escarpment. For the next few thousand years, five *separate* "Niagara Falls," all within a few miles of each other, tumbled over that cliff. Today, only a single magnificent cataract remains.

Three centuries ago, the Franciscan priest Louis Hennepin, chaplain of Robert Cavalier sieur de La Salle's expedition to explore the Mississippi River, was the first European to be led to the falls by native Americans. With the exception of the Alps, there were few natural wonders in Europe to prepare Hennepin for this colossal cascade. From the moment of his "discovery," the grandeur and beauty of this great spectacle placed Niagara Falls at the top of everyone's sightseeing wish-list.

Draining the largest (quarter-million square mile) fresh-water lake basin in the world, the Niagara River is more of a strait than a stream. It is only 33 miles long, with Lake Erie as its sole major tributary. In one astounding 176-foot splash, it carries the beautiful sediment-free overflow of four of the Great Lakes (HMES) down into the Niagara Gorge and out into Lake Ontario.

You can see and hear the geologic clock tick at Niagara Falls. On the Canadian side, as a hundred million gallons of water a minute erode the caprock, chunks of Horseshoe Falls regularly break off and tumble into the plunge pool below---a pool as deep as the falls are high.

The actual lip of the falls at which Father Hennepin stared in amazement in 1678, part of a bed of resistant 80-foot-thick dolomite, has long since eroded back; in the intervening 300 years Niagara Falls has traveled a thousand feet upstream.

The drainage pattern, too, is changing. Barring some hydraulic diversion, visitors a century hence will be able to walk over the bed of the Niagara River to Goat Island. The American Falls will be dry, and the Horseshoe Falls, already receiving 90% of Niagara River water, will be more spectacular than ever.

For 16 years, until it was retired in 1938 by a bust of William McKinley, this handsome 25¢ stamp (#568) reminded everyone with overweight mail and parcels, of the beautiful land in which we live.

DLIFE CONSERVA

D TURKEY

NITED STATES POSTA

THE INHABITANTS

#1077

#C23

On the same day that Congress signed the declaration that forever separated the United States from Great Britain, it also appointed a special committee---Thomas Jefferson, John Adams, and Benjamin Franklin---to choose an emblem for the new nation. Should it be a bird? There were 648 North American species to choose from.

What happened in that committee? Did Tom and John actually outvote Ben and choose *Haliaeetus leucocephalus*, the bald eagle (#C23, C48), instead of Franklin's "much more respectable" wild turkey (#1077)? If John had voted with Ben (who felt the eagle had "*a bad moral character*"), would we now be stuffing our National Bird into the oven each Thanksgiving? But more pressing problems quickly took those three Founding Fathers off the case.

During the next seven years, that responsibility for choosing an emblem and a seal passed from one Congressional committee to another. By 1782, Congress found itself relying on the talents of William Barton, an amateur heraldic designer from Philadelphia. He produced, among several other sketches, a rather scrawny-looking bald eagle, which he proclaimed as "*the Symbol of Supreme Power and Authority, signifying the Congress.*"

Congress's Secretary Charles Thomson revised Barton's effort, and on June 20, 1782 the United States finally had its "*Great Seal.*" Thirteen stars float above the bald eagle's head. Thirteen stripes form a shield on its breast. Gripped in its beak is a Thomson contribution, a ribbon lettered "*E Pluribus Unum*"--- "from the many, one." In one claw, an olive branch, for the nation's love of peace; in the other, 13 arrows, for the colonies' original willingness to fight for freedoms held dear.

Today, more than 200 years later, while the bald eagle still soars majestically across the American imagination, our national emblem has actually become an endangered species. Once-abundant bald eagles are now so scarce in the Lower 48 that in some states the sight of an eagle can be a birdwatching event. Only recently has the United States begun to augment, rather than diminish, the bald eagle's chances for survival in the country it has served so long and faithfully as an emblem.

In that one heartwarming development may be more symbolism than Tom and John and Ben ever dreamed possible.

#C48

#1077

KING
SALMON

#287

We took away their country.

We began by taking away their name. They had always called themselves "People of the Way." We told them they were *"Indians"* (#565).

"Our manifest destiny," proclaimed John Louis O'Sullivan in the *United States Magazine and Democratic Review* in 1845, *"is to o'erspread this continent, allotted to us by Providence for the free development of our yearly multiplying millions."* But long before O'Sullivan coined his elegant geopolitical phrase, early North American settlers had embarked on a long and bitter struggle to displace the original inhabitants.

It took three centuries for whites in this "sweet and alien land" to multiply from zero to more than two hundred million---while the Native American population dropped by half.

The American Revolution altered nothing but the rhetoric. Glowing promises made to Native Americans in the Northwest Territory Ordinance of 1787---*"their lands and property shall never be taken from them without their consent"*---were soon forgotten in the Indian Removal Act of 1830.

During his first administration, Thomas Jefferson gathered more Native American land under the skirts of the United States than any other president. "We will never do an unjust act to you," he assured its native owners, "We wish you to live in peace, possessed of your property, protected by regular laws. Our people look upon you as brethren, born in the same land and having the same interests."

But traders and land speculators, dispensing alcohol and cheap trinkets, deemed otherwise. By 1830 de Tocqueville could note how American natives were *"now isolated in their own country, a little colony of troublesome strangers in the midst of a numerous and dominant people."*

Today, with the exception of those Native Americans who have somehow managed to remain in control of their own "manifest destiny," most are relegated to a marginal existence on the social and cultural edge of America. Many are immigrants in their own country, drawn by promises of education and jobs from whatever is left of a once-proud domain, to urban underclass areas with inevitable poverty, poor health, alcoholism, and malaise.

USA 15

#2178

We used to call this magnificent, strangely humped, heavily mantled creature (#569) a "buffalo." The word came trippingly to the tongue---can you imagine anyone ever referring to the flamboyant Wild West showman (#2178) as "Bison Bill"?

The American bison---its correct name---is huge and ponderous, with baleful eye. It shares a spot in the ox family tree with its European cousin, the aurochs.

Millennia before there were native Americans (#287) seeking meat and hides, crawling with their bows and arrows through the high prairie grass, millions of bison roamed peacefully across much of our continent, darkening the Great Plains with herds so vast they took hours to pass a given point.

Unfortunately for these large and mainly passive ox family members on both sides of the Atlantic, in the 19th century they were cruelly hunted down for sport---almost to the edge of extinction.

An early American plainsman tells a tale of such senseless slaughter: "That morning one of the hunters had ungenerously objected to sharing a buffalo with Mr. W., whereupon Mr. W. set out vowing to kill one for himself, and no thanks to anyone. He had not been out long when he spied a herd of seven bulls, quietly feeding near a ravine. Slipping up behind the bank, he shot down one and then another, until they all lay before him. Their seven tongues he brought in, swung to his saddle, as testimony to his skill with a gun."

Soon there were only two tiny bison herds in all of North America---at Yellowstone Park and in Canada. Spurred by the enlightened efforts of the American Bison Society, the time seemed ripe for some level of government intervention and preservation.

In 1894, more than 20 years after the establishment of Yellowstone, the U.S. Department of Interior forbade killing any more bison in the park. Very slowly, in newly established national refuges across the Northwest, the once-great bison herds slowly recovered---to become living symbols of our former vast American wilderness. Overseas, too, a few remaining aurochs still graze peacefully in carefully protected Eastern European reserves.

But we all came close.

#569

#1889A

It would have been a pity to lose the whooping crane (#1098). In 1941, after 50 million years, there were only as many whooping cranes left in the world as stamps on the next page.

Unique to North America, the five-foot-high whooping cranes are the continent's tallest birds. Throughout the ages, they have carried on elaborate and noisy courtship rituals, with much wild trumpeting, wing flapping, head bowing, and huge aerial leaps. The mating event usually results in two eggs, but a pair of cranes rarely succeeds in raising more than a single chick to maturity---hardly a formula for avian overpopulation.

As the United States expanded, land development and rural electrification placed enormous pressure on the whooping cranes' migration route---2,500 miles a year back and forth from the salt marshes and tidal flats of the south Texas coast to some unknown spot in northern Canada. Collision with power lines became a major problem; callous hunters took their toll. By the beginning of this century, whooping cranes in captivity were living twice as long as those in the wild.

Worst of all, the wetlands on which migrating and wintering cranes relied for food and nesting sites were being rapidly converted into dry farmland. Before the whooping crane became as extinct as the passenger pigeon and heath hen, immediate action was necessary.

In the summer of 1954, a bush pilot flying over a remote section of northeastern Alberta finally discovered the whooping crane's summer breeding grounds. As the United States became more "crane conscious" and numbers slowly increased, Fish & Wildlife scientists were inspired to fly "spare" eggs down from Canada, to build three new backup flocks.

Two flocks have already become successful captive groups in Maryland and Wisconsin. Eggs were also substituted in *sandhill* crane nests in northern Idaho; the more prolific sandhills became unsuspecting foster parents. A dozen or so Idaho whooping cranes have accepted the shorter sandhill winter flyway to New Mexico---but refuse to breed.

Today's wild North American whooping cranes have now been shifted from the "endangered" to the "threatened" species list. Even that slight improvement makes the whooping crane a heartwarming international symbol of wildlife conservation.

THE EXPLORERS

In fourteen hundred and ninety-two
Columbus sailed the ocean blue…

But any schoolchild can tell you that the Vikings got here first, half a millennium before the great navigator from Genoa.

All anyone actually knows about those early Scandinavian sea warriors and their exploration of the North American coastline comes from a pair of sagas in the *Flateyjarbok*, written down in the 1300s from ancient oral histories. They go like this:

Bjarni Herjolfsson, blown west from Iceland by a terrible storm, after many days at sea encounters a flat, inhospitable land. He beats his way slowly back to Greenland. In 1001 A.D., Bjarni sells his vessel to Leifr Eiriksson, son of Eric the Red. Eiriksson also sails west and discovers Heulluland, "land of stones"; Markland, "land of forests"; and Vinland, "land of grapes." A few years later, Eiriksson's brothers Thorvald and Thorstein make the same exploration, followed in 1020 by Thorfinn Karlsefni, who conducts an extensive coastal reconnaissance.

That's all there is. Nothing more.

The supportive evidence is both real and imagined. The most recent flap has been over *"Friar Carpani's 1440 Vinland Map"*---unearthed at Yale University in 1965. It mentions Eiriksson. With uncanny accuracy it traces a section of the North American coastline. But in less than a decade, researchers discovered Carpani's ink contains *anatase*, a titanium compound synthesized 500 years after the good Father's demise.

All we can truly say about Viking probes into the New World so long before Columbus is this: if the Vikings came ashore in North America, they didn't stay very long. They soon sought elsewhere for more promising and less hazardous lands to explore, conquer, and settle.

The Vikings were Norsemen, Swedes and Danes. Hence a Viking ship is pictured on this stamp *(#621)*, which celebrates the 100th anniversary of the arrival in New York harbor of a group of Norwegian immigrants. It's one more example of the way those dragon-prowed vessels come running down to us before the misty winds of our imagination, their horn-helmeted captains poking into all the rocky inlets and twisting creeks from Labrador to Narragansett Bay.

#245

The history of the world has been a history of continued expansion, resulting from population and economic pressures, famine, epidemics, and religious and political persecution. That expansion has also reflected man's overwhelming desire to see what lies beyond the horizon, a desire customarily coupled with what Samuel Johnson once called *"the potentiality of growing rich beyond the dreams of avarice."*

Cristoforo Columbo was no exception. As proper reward for gathering the wealth of undiscovered lands for the Spanish crown, this persistent Genoese demanded a noble Spanish title, a coat of arms, high offices, and substantial personal revenues.

Sending Columbus and his 88-man crew off on a three-ship, 36-day sail down the trade winds to "The Indies" and return, was expensive. It cost $14,000, but you can ignore that hoary old chestnut about Queen Isabella bringing her jewels to the pawnshop; the Spanish court was far wealthier than *that*.

The fact that Their Most Serene Spanish Highnesses finally signed Columbus's rigorous contract was due to four influential courtiers: the Dominican priest Diego de Deza of Salamanca (later Archbishop of Seville); Juan Cabrero, the royal chamberlain; Raphael Sanchez, the royal treasurer; and Luis de Santangel, King Ferdinand's keeper of the privy purse, to whom Columbus dispatched the very first letter joyfully announcing his discovery of a new world.

Those four were all devout Spanish Catholics of Jewish descent, who believed that the key to the wealth of the Indies, soon to fuel the most magnificent era of Spanish history, lay beyond the western, not the eastern, horizon. From the religious antecedents of these four important backers comes the apparently inextinguishable belief that the explorer himself was Jewish.

All that history can tell us about that conjecture is "not proven." But one thing makes the religious background of those four enthusiastic supporters particularly ironic. On the very day that Columbus set sail from Palos, all practicing Spanish Jews were expelled from Spain.

Although Columbus's explorations in quest of fame and fortune carried him nowhere near the present borders of the United States, our country was the first in the hemisphere to celebrate the momentous landing on San Salvador (*#231*).

Slightly over four centuries after that original October 12, on the occasion of Chicago's great World's Columbian Exposition, the Post Office issued its first true U.S. commemorative stamps.

#230

Sixteen of these tiny tableaux were printed for the government by the American Bank Note Company. During part of the run, the pressman inked the 4¢ plate---*Fleet of Columbus* --- with blue ink, instead of ultramarine, thereby increasing the present value of a cancelled example more than four hundred fold.

Like a movie trailer, those famous *"Columbians"* trace in denominational disorder the entire canon of his discovery:

Columbus (#245)
Columbus at La Rabida
Isabella and Columbus
Columbus Soliciting Aid of Isabella
Recall of Columbus
Isabella Pledging Her Jewels
Fleet of Columbus
Flag Ship of Columbus (#232)
Columbus in Sight of Land (#230)
Landing of Columbus (#231)
Columbus Welcomed at Barcelona
Columbus Announcing His Discovery
Columbus Presenting Indians
Columbus in Chains
Columbus Restored to Favor
Columbus Describing Third Voyage.

This 16-stamp series that launched the United States "commemorative era" may seem like postal overkill, but the Chicago fair was world class; 72 nations participated. In the six months that the great "White City" stood on the shores of Lake Michigan, unlocking creative energies in a host of fields, it attracted 27 million visitors. It is perhaps best remembered for its eclectic mix of Greek, Renaissance, Romanesque, and modern architectural styles---as well as for Little Egypt's unprecedented "hootchy-kootchy" dance on the midway.

"The Admiral of the Ocean Sea" would have been delighted with all the hoopla.

#U348

In the dozen years that followed the discovery of the Bahamas, Cuba, and Santo Domingo, Columbus made three more voyages to the New World. Always seeking a direct route to *"The Indies,"* still believing he was near a channel to the Malay Peninsula, Columbus visited many other Caribbean islands, sighted the South American mainland, and finally coasted along the shores of Central America from Honduras to Panama.

Meanwhile Portuguese explorers and adventurers were not idle; Pope Alexander IV soon found it expedient to separate Spanish and Portuguese claims to lands in the New World by drawing a longitudinal line down the Atlantic 300 miles west of the Azores and Cape Verde Islands. This was soon adjusted 800 additional miles westward, to put the east coast of South America under Portuguese control.

The French and English cared nary a whit for the Pope's paper line. They not only dispatched voyages of exploration all over the east coast of North America, but were soon trespassing in waters and lands that the Spanish, by right of discovery and papal pronouncement, had claimed as their own.

In one of the world's great sonnets, John Keats, after "First Looking Into Chapman's *Homer*," compares himself to *"Stout Cortez…with eagle eyes…silent upon a peak in Darien."* Keats was a wonderful poet but a poor historian. The man who first crossed the Isthmus to that Panama mountaintop to stare silently out over the Pacific was not the great Hernan Cortés, but an easygoing Spanish *conquistador* named Vasco Núñez de Balboa.

Four hundred years later the United States government, celebrating our soon-to-be-opened Panama Canal, helped straighten out Keats's error. It devoted a stamp (#397) to Balboa, real discoverer of the eastern Pacific Ocean, a man lured across the Isthmus by native tales of a "Great South Sea."

Zuni natives in the Southwest played a trick on Franciscan missionary Marcos de Niza. They fed him tall tales of pueblos crammed with gold, silver, and precious stones---the "Seven Cities of Cibola." In 1540, fired by de Niza's reports, the 30-year-old governor of *Nueva Galicia*, Francisco Vásquez de Coronado, set off on an expedition (#898) with de Niza as his guide.

#397

Captain-General Coronado and several parties under his command spent almost three years tramping up and down two thousand miles of native trails between Mexico and Kansas, looking for those chimerical Cibolan riches; Coronado finally sent de Niza home in disgrace.

Meanwhile, a detachment under Garcia López de Cárdenas discovered the Grand Canyon, and a naval arm of the expedition, commanded by Hernando de Alarcón, sailed hundreds of miles up the Gulf of California to the mouth of the Colorado River.

#898

❧

Rambunctious Francis Drake probably covered more sea miles than any other Englishman afloat. In 1577, the 36-year-old Drake commanded five ships and 160 sailors on a freebooting voyage along the west coast of South America, sacking Spanish towns and seizing treasure galleons. Drake left such devastation in his wake that it became unwise for him to retrace his steps. He sailed home to London the hard way---*around the world.*

En route Drake paused long enough in San Francisco Bay (#400a) to refit his sole remaining ship, the *Golden Hind.* He supposedly left behind a brass plate announcing that the entire California coast---*New Albion*---now belonged to Elizabeth I. After a four-year absence Drake returned to England, carrying booty worth half a million pounds. The Queen gave him a knighthood. Eight years later he destroyed the Spanish Armada.

❧

Père Jacques Marquette was a Jesuit missionary with a flair for languages. In 1666 he came to New France to minister to the native tribes around Lake Superior. He was intrigued with their stories of a great waterway that flowed not west, but south, all the way to the Gulf of Mexico. Governor Frontenac granted him permission to investigate.

#400a

In 1673 the 36-year-old priest set off in a pair of canoes with the well-educated, Canadian-born Louis Joliet, and five *voyageurs*, to explore all the tributaries of the upper Mississippi River (#285). Marquette's ability to speak local native dialects assured success for this momentous four-month, 2,500-mile expedition that opened the upper Midwest to French traders. Nine years later Robert Cavalier sieur de La Salle descended the Mississippi, all the way to its mouth.

#285

THE COLONIZERS

Almost a century after Columbus, navigators Philip Amadas and Arthur Barlowe were cruising the Carolina coast on behalf of Sir Walter Raleigh, poking into likely spots where the governor might exercise his royal patent to establish a colony in the "heathen lands" of North America. *"I shall yet live to see this an Inglishe nation,"* Raleigh wrote prophetically.

Returning to London, the two captains told Raleigh of a pleasant and fertile island the natives called *"Roanoke,"* in Pamlico Sound, 45 miles north of Cape Hatteras.

In April 1585 Raleigh dispatched several hundred soldiers with 100 colonists in seven ships commanded by his cousin Sir Philip Grenville. The fleet paused at Roanoke Island long enough to deposit the settlers in a hastily-constructed fort with outbuildings, dutifully named "The Citie of Ralegh."

Without any help from local natives, only a tiny handful of starving men outlasted the winter. In the spring, Sir Francis Drake swooped in and carried them all back to England.

In July 1587 Raleigh sent out another expedition, this time led by his deputy governor John White---who earlier had made marvelous drawings of the abundant native agriculture on the mainland of *"Virginia,"* named after the virgin queen. Raleigh had learned from experience: this time his colonists would treat *"the naturall people with all humanitie, curtesie, and freedom."*

White's orders were to settle along the headwaters of Chesapeake Bay; instead he sailed again to Roanoke. His fleet carried 150 settlers, including 17 women. Among them was White's eight-months-pregnant daughter Ellinor Dare.

White arrived far too late in the season to plant any seed. Before long, sickness was increasing and food was running low. White took the group's remaining ship and sailed home for help.

But England was preparing for the Spanish Armada of 1588. White's own return to Roanoke was delayed for almost four years; the two relief ships he immediately sent out turned around to pillage the Spanish coast.

When White finally got back to Roanoke in 1591, the entire colony, including his daughter---and granddaughter Virginia (#796)---had disappeared.

The only clue was four letters, *"CROA"*---perhaps for "Croatoan," a friendly local native tribe---carved into a tree.

5 POSTAGE 5 CENTS

In memory of
Born Roanoke 1587
Virginia Dare

#328

For an Elizabethan age crammed with biographers, it seems strange that the only contemporary authority on John Smith is the good Captain himself (#328). Hardly bashful, Smith wrote a dozen books, most of which appear to be true, about his amazing adventures and hairbreadth escapes.

Everyone knows how Smith's life was saved by 12-year-old Princess Pocahontas (#330) who dove under the club of her father, Chief Powhatan. But that bit of schoolyard history is only sideshow compared to all the other remarkable achievements of the man who almost singlehandedly *WILLED* the British colonization of North America.

Courageous, resourceful, reliable John Smith poured his heart, soul, and whatever money he possessed into one big idea---the Virginia Company. He helped obtain its charter from James I, and in the spring of 1607, sailed off to the New World with more than a hundred other "English gentlemen" on his greatest personal and business adventure (#329).

Fewer than 40 colonists survived that first Jamestown winter, kept alive only by Smith's desperate trades for food with Chief Powhatan. Again and again Smith wrote home: Virginia can succeed only if it becomes self-sufficient, free of the steady stream of supply ships from London.

Replied the Company: "Use your gentlemen to dig gold."

On both sides of the Atlantic, resentment grew. By the summer of 1609, despite all of Smith's energetic accomplishments, the Company's financiers summoned the great colonizer home---he never again returned to Virginia. Without Smith, the following winter of want is still remembered in the Old Dominion as "The Starving Time." Only a providential group of relief ships saved the colony from extinction.

Back in England, Smith immediately set himself up as the 17th century equivalent of an exploration consultant. By then he was a ripe 29 years old; everything he did breathed enthusiasm. During Smith's last summer in the New World, his old friend Henry Hudson was tacking back and forth off the Virginia Capes. If Hudson had considered coming ashore to ask Smith if he had any clues as to the true location of the mythical "Northwest Passage," John would probably have dropped everything---and helped Henry find the darn thing.

#329

#548

It was an inauspicious beginning for a reasonably well-financed effort to establish the first religious commonwealth in North America. Aboard the leaky little 60-ton *Speedwell* and the heavier three-masted *Mayflower* were a handful of Church of England Separatists---godly farmers and artisans from Scrooby in Nottinghamshire, by way of Leiden in Holland.

The passengers called themselves "*Puritans*," because they wished to purify the rites and discipline of the Church of England through a direct covenant with God. They had fled from the mockery and criticism of their conforming neighbors, and spent a dozen years of self-exile in the easygoing university city of Leiden, until congregation leaders feared members were backsliding into "unregenerate Dutch corruption."

Business contacts with less dogmatic Puritans within the Virginia Company helped the Leiden group obtain a royal patent from King James for a new English settlement in Virginia. Despite stiff terms of a traditional seven-year labor indenture, the bolder spirits in Leiden were soon selling their property and purchasing stock for a plantation company that could provide clothing, agricultural tools, and supplies---and charter the necessary ships to carry the dissenters across the Atlantic.

Eventually, more than half the Leiden group decided to stay put where they were in Holland. The "*Pilgrim*" minority moved on to England to negotiate a final contract.

On August 5, 1620, quite late in the year to plant seed in the New World, the unseaworthy *Speedwell* and the *Mayflower* finally set sail from Southampton---presumably headed for the Virginia coast.

But soon the two ships were back in England, where several families from the *Speedwell* abandoned the trip. On September 16 the double-decked *Mayflower* (#548) alone headed westward, carrying 24 families and their servants, with ten single men. Of the 101 passengers aboard, only 37 were the chosen elect of Leiden; the rest were ordinary emigrants the Pilgrims called "*Strangers*." In addition, some orphans had been "picked up" off the streets of London to act as the Pilgrims' body servants.

Two months later, after the long confinement of an arduous voyage with wretched provisions, the *Mayflower* finally made a landfall off the uninviting shores of Cape Cod (#549).

#682

With permanent settlements at Jamestown and Plimouth (Plymouth) Plantation assured, the remainder of the British-held North American seaboard appeared ready for intensive development.

But with Plimouth established, where else could other Puritans go? In 1622, a fishing station known as the Dorchester Company was established by English West Country merchants on Cape Ann, 40 miles north of Plimouth. Failing after five years, the station was taken over by the New England Company, a commercial group composed mainly of East Anglian Puritans. They reorganized themselves a year later into *"The Governor and Company of the* MASSACHUSETTS *Bay in New England"*---named by the stockholders after the native Algonquian tribe the Puritans would soon displace.

Originated by a Council for New England patent in 1629, the Massachusetts Bay Company charter was quickly confirmed through royal grant (#682). Whether by oversight or design, the commercial charter did not contain the usual requirement that *the company maintain its headquarters in England.*

Charter in hand, the Puritan leaders moved swiftly to make eastern Massachusetts an economic and political haven---not just for a handful of Pilgrims, but for the entire English Puritan sect. Once their intention was evident, the London Council for New England attempted to annul the royal grant---but it was too late.

A tide of enthusiastic Puritan emigration---900 settlers on 11 ships in 1630 alone, 20,000 by 1642---swept company, charter, and a belief in independent government straight through Salem and Charlestown, to what soon became the pre-eminent town in Massachusetts, Boston. There the Puritans, in a remarkable feat of early American business prestidigitation, transformed their commercial company into a sovereign religious commonwealth, with some aspects of political democracy.

But the austere Puritan elders who had chafed under Anglican persecution at home, now became equally inflexible and intolerant abroad. Any whisper of dissent in the new commonwealth was viewed as the voice of the Devil. The witch-hunt smell of sulphur and brimstone tainted the air.

Before long the colony was losing some of its most eminent men and women---by banishment.

The most fearlessly outspoken Puritan, a man who placed a high value on personal liberty, was Roger Williams. For his radical assertion that civil government possessed no authority over spiritual offense, as well as his disquieting insistence that valid land titles could only come from the natives, not from the King, this young, well-educated teacher of the Salem church was tried and banished in 1635 by the General Court (legislature) of Massachusetts Bay Colony.

#777

Escaping a last-minute kidnap attempt to ship him back to England, Williams fled 40 miles south through the New England woods, where he purchased bayshore land from the native Narragansett chiefs. There Williams founded the heterodox settlement he called "*Providence Plantations*"---after "God's merciful providence" (#777).

Unlike Massachusetts, Providence Plantations was a place where civil magistrates held no sway over matters of conscience. In his vigorous, controversial writings, Williams expounded many democratic and humanitarian ideas. His cardinal principle was absolute liberty for every form of religious expression; the little colony even welcomed Quakers and Jews.

By now Williams was a Christian without creed, whose path through the wilderness was quickly followed by other disputatious exiles and self-exiles from Massachusetts Bay Colony. As might be expected from such a group of free spirits suddenly set loose, there ensued a long and often bitter history of town infighting.

But local and doctrinal animosities were brushed aside when Massachusetts Bay Colony and Plimouth Plantation, who viewed the growing success of their upstart neighbor with fear and loathing, laid political claim to the region they sneeringly called "*Rogue's Island.*"

#1099

Williams and the other settlers struck back, enlisting the aid of influential friends in England. In 1644 they secured a patent to their lands from Cromwell's Long Parliament. A civil code was established and a permanent government organized.

In 1663, a royal charter from Charles II finally confirmed to the rest of British North America that the fiercely independent colony of "*Rhode Island and Providence Plantations in the Narragansett Bay*" was definitely here to stay.

By rights Connecticut should be Dutch. Adriaen Block of Nieu Nederlandt sailed up the Connecticut River long before the Pilgrims in Holland ever considered seeking an American haven. When a group from Plimouth Plantation finally came prowling through the Connecticut valley in 1632, the Dutch quickly built a fort on the river. But it hardly proved an obstacle to the wave of settlers who eventually swept into those wide, lush meadows during the Great Puritan Migration. Three Massachusetts towns ---Watertown, Dorchester, and Cambridge---actually moved *en masse* to the more fertile soil of Connecticut; some newcomers even built homes around the "alien" fort. After a quarter century, the outnumbered Dutch took the hint and departed.

Local Puritan autonomy was established in 1635, with the blessing of the Bay Colony---the new settlements were orthodox copies of those in Massachusetts. Four years later representatives of the three new major Connecticut towns met at Hartford and confirmed the *"Fundamental Orders"* for a theocratic government of substantial, respectable male Christians. Forty-five "blue laws" were adopted, prohibiting, among other things, trial by jury. They also decreed death for adultery, with jail terms for concealing Quakers.

In 1662, the *Orders* were replaced with slight change by a royal charter from Charles II, which gave the colony its first legal standing. In 1687 a governor general of New England came to Hartford to demand physical surrender of the royal charter. Tradition insists the legislature snuffed out its candles, whisked the document out the window, and hid it in the trunk of a huge hollow white oak. The "Charter Oak" (*#772*) stood until 1856 as a revered symbol of early colonial resistance to tyranny.

❧

In 1609 Henry Hudson sailed up the broad and unknown river that henceforth bore his name. For a moment the free-lance English explorer thought he had finally found the mythical "Northwest Passage."

Hudson was under contract to the Netherlands East India Company, so for 15 years only Dutch traders were permitted to sail into the magnificent harbor that surrounded the island home of the Algonquian *Manhates* tribe. It was not until 1624 that the Dutch felt sufficiently secure in their long war of independence

#1027

from Spain to purchase from the natives, for a handful of trinkets, the right to establish a permanent settlement on Manhattan Island. A year earlier 30 families of Huguenot Walloon refugees from southern Holland crossed the Atlantic on the *Nieu Nederlandt*, and settled upriver at Fort Orange (*#615*). In 1653, governor Pieter Stuyvesant declared the little Dutch town a municipality (*#1027*). By then the colony was being elbowed by its English neighbors. In 1664 four Royal Navy frigates showed up off Fort Amsterdam, trained their guns on the town's quaint stone houses, and announced to the startled burghers that the end had come---Nieu Nederlandt was now split into two British colonies: "*New York*" and "*New Jersey*."

"*In tyme,*"announced the new English governor, "*we shall fill this vacant wildernesse with plantations of His Majtys subjects.*" Which very quickly happened.

During the first half of the 17th century, possession of the area that is now Pennsylvania was disputed by the Swedes, Dutch, and English. The 1643 New Sweden settlements of Upland and New Gottenberg, peopled mainly by Finns (#836), lasted only a dozen years. They were seized in 1655 by Pieter Stuyvesant, who asserted Dutch sovereignty.

Stuyvesant's rule lasted only until 1664, when the entire region, together with "*New York*" and "*New Jersey,*" was taken over by the British. At that time, William Penn (*#724*) was only 20 years old, recently expelled from Oxford for over-zealous exercise of his religious scruples. He would soon become a member of the peaceful Society of Friends---a "*Quaker.*" His father (also William Penn) was a distinguished admiral in the Royal Navy. Not nominally a royalist, the admiral had secretly assisted in the restoration of Charles II, for which the king owed the elder Penn a large figurative---and even larger monetary--- debt. He was quickly knighted.

For the next 18 years, during which time his father died, young William Penn, prolifically writing religious tracts, found himself in and out of various minor government sinecures---and jail. He continued to dream of using the king's debt to help create a "Holy Experiment," a home for his co-religionists, similar to the haven the Puritans were enjoying up in Massachusetts.

#724

#836

#615

1624

HUGUENOT WALLO

2

C

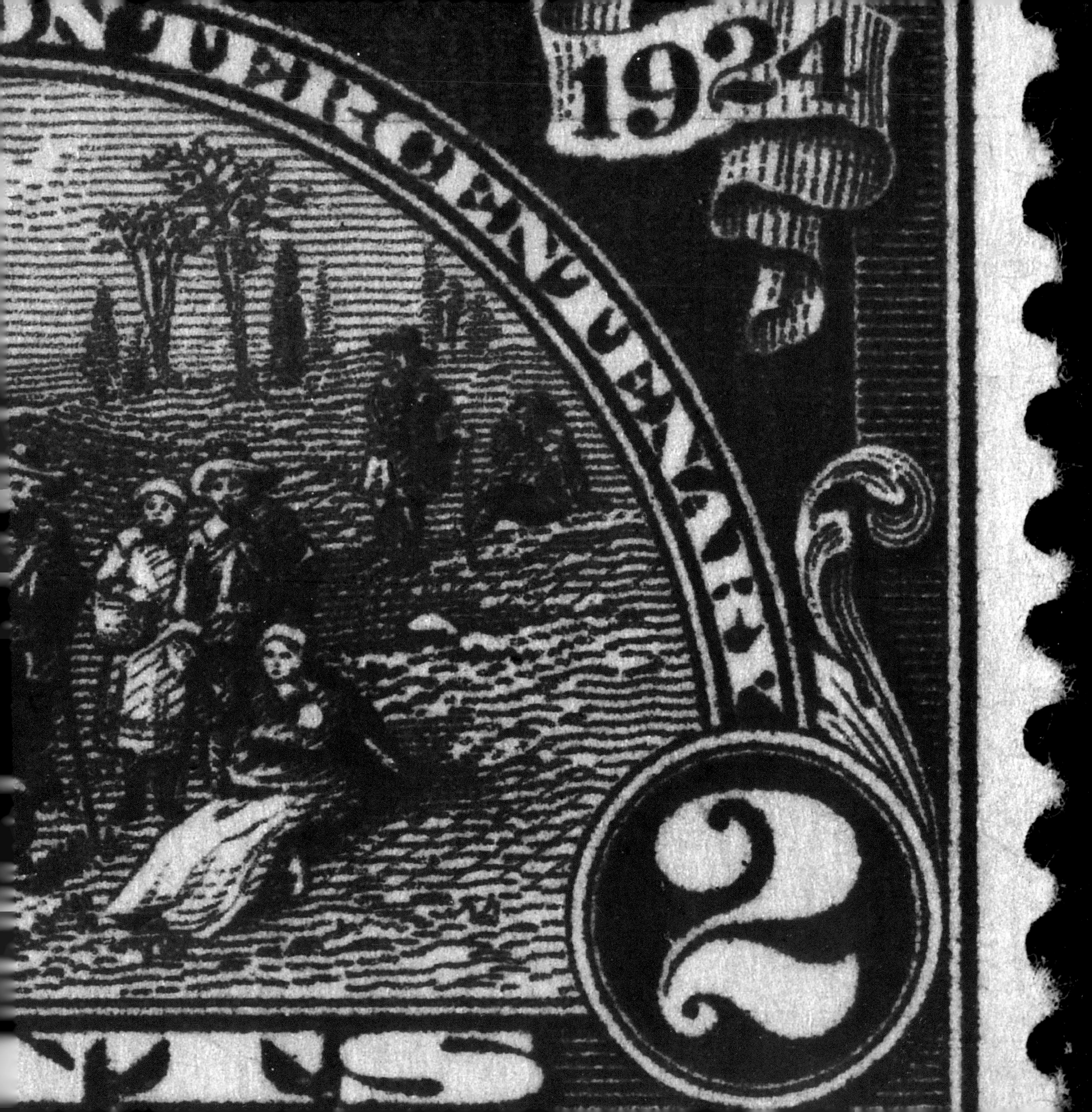
1924
2

#736

In 1680 Penn petitioned Charles II, and received, in lieu of monies owed, title to a 48,000-square-mile area between Maryland and New York, plus a lease on three lower counties that later became the colony of Delaware. In honor of the late admiral, the king himself named the new colony "*Pennsylvania---Penn's woods*": the always modest Penn strove unsuccessfully to remove his name from the title.

The proprietor's rights under the charter were almost unlimited. Penn's watchword, unusual for those times, was friendly relations with the natives. He wrote a democratic *Frame of Government*, and in 1682, finally sailed for America with 100 Friends on the good ship *Welcome*, to lay out a "great town"---the "*City of Brotherly Love*"---Philadelphia.

The Society of Friends had finally found a place of its own in America; in two years, Philadelphia could boast 2,500 inhabitants.

❦

Cecilius Calvert, the second Lord Baltimore, absolute lord and proprietor of Maryland, set a regal tone for the landed English gentry in the colonies. For 60 years the Calvert family ruled over a seven-million-acre estate surrounding Chesapeake Bay, granted by Charles I and named in honor of the queen consort. Calvert's father was a convert to Catholicism, and Cecilius's brother Leonard, serving as the colony's first governor, originally wished to people Maryland with co-religionists. But in 1634, the first two shiploads of 200 settlers aboard the *Ark* and *Dove* (#736) must have been a disappointment to Leonard. The majority of them were Protestant weavers, tradesmen, impoverished tenant farmers, and laborers---along with a sprinkling of vagrants, orphans, petty criminals, and prostitutes.

❦

In the Carolinas in 1663, empire-building was carried to new extremes. Charles II gave eight favorite courtiers all the land between Virginia and Florida from the Atlantic to the Pacific Oceans (#683)---600 *million acres*. The lucky eight included the Earl of Shaftesbury, and General George Monck, a turncoat from Cromwell's Parliamentary Army. The Earl's secretary John Locke drafted a *Fundamental Constitution* for the Carolinas. In years to come, Locke's famous ideas about the "social contract" between

#683

governors and those they governed would influence the men who wrote the Declaration of Independence and the Constitution.

#726

Georgia was the last English colony established in North America. Originally part of the Carolinas, it included an area over which the Spanish explorer Ferdinando de Soto had marched in 1540, seeking gold. This led to continuous land squabbles with Spain, from which the Carolina proprietors usually backed away. In 1732, England decided to establish a separate military buffer colony between the Carolinas and Spanish Florida. George II granted a 21-year charter---and Parliament gave £10,000 seed money---to General James Oglethorpe (#726), a young philanthropic member of Commons, who was also an authority on penal conditions in England.

Oglethorpe and his trustee/associates named their new non-profit colony after the King, establishing it as a catch-all asylum for persecuted European Protestant sects and imprisoned English debtors. One hundred and sixteen immigrants, mainly refugees from continental Europe, sailed with Oglethorpe in 1733 to establish Savannah, Georgia's first settlement. Strong liquor, Catholics, slaves, and immigrants from any other colony were banned.

Before long, Oglethorpe had decisively defeated the Florida Spanish. He then required all his Georgia immigrants to plant grapes, hemp, and medicinal plants, as well as mulberry trees to satisfy the English need for silk. The result was a sorry agricultural disappointment, and Oglethorpe's rigid rule soon led to his recall. When his charter expired in 1754, Georgia became a crown colony, whereupon its new rice-growing *laissez-faire* economy boomed, making the colony a somewhat lukewarm participant in the First and Second Continental Congresses and the War of the Revolution.

Throughout the English colonies of North America, misrule, improper development, plus the failure to address the real economic and political aspirations of the inhabitants, sooner or later brought an end to "private governments" wherever they existed. Original grants and charters were revoked, and colonial administration returned to the British crown.

THE REVOLUTIONARIES

#629

The ultimate weapon in the Revolutionary armory was the colonial printing press. In the contest for what John Adams would describe as "*the principles, opinions, sentiments, and affections of the American people,*" an unending stream of royal and revolutionary newspapers, pamphlets, cartoons, broadsides, books, and even ballads flowed for decades from these dirty, heavy, cumbersome, but ingenious wood-and-metal devices.

The first printing press to come to America (#857), accompanied by several fonts of Roman type and a large quantity of Dutch printing paper, was earmarked for Harvard College. It was all purchased in England in 1637 for that new "academy" in Cambridge, Massachusetts, by the Reverend John Glover, a wealthy English Puritan.

Sadly, Glover died while accompanying the press to Boston (his widow married the first president of Harvard). In 1810 the famous American printer Isaiah Thomas recounted Glover's pioneer effort, praising him as "one of the best and firmest friends to New England." It would be more than 40 years before printing gained a foothold elsewhere on the Atlantic seaboard.

It was left to Glover's master workman Stephen Daye, who traveled with the cleric, to inaugurate the press at Cambridge in 1639 with *The Freeman's Oath*---the first piece of paper printed in British North America. Daye was a member of a prominent London printing family; his importance to the New England community was immediately recognized. The Bay Colony awarded him "three hundred Acres of Land in any place not formerly Graunted...for Recompense of his Care and Charg in furthering the worke of Printing."

In 1639, Daye and his Harvard press issued the first book printed in the colonies, with the run-on title *The Psalms in Metre, Faithfully translated for the Use, Edification, and Comfort of the Saints in Public and Private, especially in New England.* Daye did not repay his benefactors with particularly high quality work. That first edition (noted Isaiah Thomas) "abounded with typographical errors...not exhibiting the appearance of good workmanship. The compositor must have been wholly unacquainted with punctuation...the spelling and hyphenation were bad and irregular."

Thomas should have been a contemporary book reviewer.

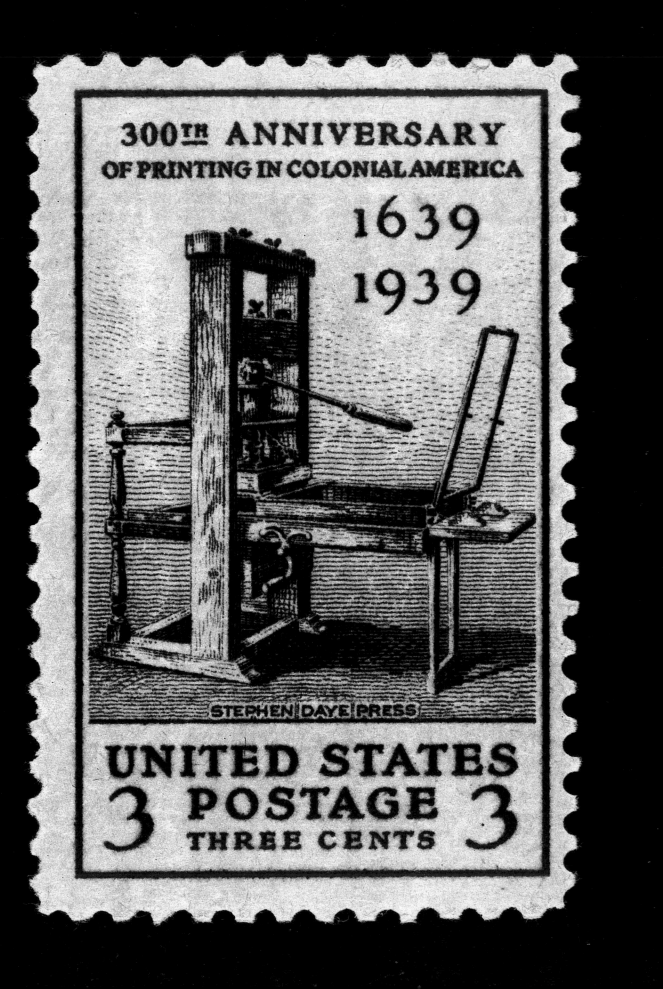

300TH ANNIVERSARY
OF PRINTING IN COLONIAL AMERICA

1639
1939

STEPHEN DAYE PRESS

UNITED STATES
3 POSTAGE 3
THREE CENTS

#1048

In the gray dawn of April 19, 1775, a small band of apprehensive Massachusetts militiamen milled about on Lexington green. A few hours earlier, Paul Revere (#1048), evading several British cavalry patrols, scurried into town to roust two important visitors, Sam Adams and John Hancock, from their beds. He brought news that 700 British infantrymen under Lieutenant Colonel Francis Smith and marine Major John Pitcairn were on the march from Boston, 16 miles away.

After a year of inactivity, those occupation troops had been ordered by General Gage to "*seize and destroy…a quantity of Ammunition, Provisions, Artillery, Tents and small Arms…collected at Concord, for the Avowed Purpose of raising and supporting a Rebellion against His Majesty.*" So far, it was a rebellion without a battle; each of the hundred-odd "Minute Men" (#619), who had drilled for months on Lexington green under Captain John Parker, was still as freeborn an Englishmen as any King's officer.

As the British troops tramped closer, Colonel Smith ordered Pitcairn (who would be killed two months later at Bunker Hill) to move ahead and seize the bridges beyond Concord. As Pitcairn's six light infantry companies came abreast of Lexington green, the 53-year-old Scots major saw 77 of Captain Parker's militiamen lined up on his right flank.

An incised granite boulder on the green allows how Parker intoned: "*Stand your ground. Don't fire unless fired upon. But if they mean to have a war, let it begin here.*" Chances are no one, including Parker, knew exactly what to say---or do.

But the sight of that handful of unfriendly musketeers angered Pitcairn. Even though the road to Concord lay wide open before them, he deployed his men against the militia, barking at the outnumbered Americans to lay down their arms and disperse. Conscious of danger, Parker's men responded by breaking ranks and beginning to edge away.

A shot whistled across the green---from whose musket we shall never know. In a moment, against orders, the entire British force was firing at the fleeing Americans (#618). Eight men were killed; nine were wounded.

"*It is needless to mention what happened afterward,*" Pitcairn reported to General Gage.

The turning point had passed.

#619

George III of England? Not just a king, but a most misunderstood and much maligned man.

Hardly a pettifogger, George William Frederick was the prototype of the modern businessman, trapped only by a trick of time amidst bumbling English county squires. George III fought them (and almost everyone else), struggling on a worldwide scale to prepare his mighty but hopelessly corrupt empire for the 19th century.

"*George, be a king,*" his German mother used to whisper to him. To his credit, George almost succeeded.

That he failed miserably in this particular part of the world was due to another modern executive, also named George---a man who employed *four* secretaries during the Revolution: two for military orders, one for letters to Congress, the fourth for personal matters.

This "other George" also served his country without pay, truly running things, giving orders left and right, and turning out a volume of statesmanlike correspondence the likes of which the world has rarely seen. If there ever was the proper person in the proper place at the proper time, it was this other George... George Washington (*#220*).

Historians tell us that, initially, Washington seemed an unlikely Congressional choice for a national military leader.

Nonsense! Congress knew exactly what it was doing when it entrusted overall command of the Continental Army (#617) to this austere, sagacious man---a leader called (flamboyantly but accurately) by one 18th century dramatist:

> *...cool, calm, and undespairing,*
> *Like a mighty beacon 'mid the waves*
> *That lights us thro' the storm.*

For eight years Washington served the American Revolution as a courageous figurehead, ingenious military strategist, consummate politician, gentleman diplomat, and much more---continually focusing and refocusing everyone's attention and energies, through seemingly endless crises, on the almost insurmountable problems of creating a brand-new country.

Thank you, George, for so much.

The more United States postage stamps we can put your picture on, the better (*#704-715*).

#220

#704 - #7

#617

CAMBRIDGE

CONCORD

1925

1

Even as far back as 1701, London's Board of Trade called the colonies' desire for independence "notorious." Fifty-six years later, Ben Franklin found it expedient, while arguing before Parliament, to deny the allegation.

And he was right. By 1776 only about a third of the three million people living along the Atlantic seaboard wished for political separation from Great Britain. Another million didn't care. The final million were dead set against it.

The revolutionaries from all classes and every part of the colonies who were willing to "*pledge their Lives, fortunes, and sacred Honor*" to the struggle for independence were possibly smarter, probably better organized, and certainly more dedicated to principles of responsible government than the subjects who remained loyal to the King.

Despite that fact, the representatives of "*the good People of these Colonies...in General Congress Assembled,*" proceeded cautiously---at first even formally declaring "*we have not raised armies with the ambitious design of separating from Great Britain and establishing independent states.*"

Then an expatriate English pamphleteer (#1292) set American minds and hearts afire; Thomas Paine's *Common Sense* went through a dozen printings in as many weeks. "*A long habit of not thinking a thing* WRONG," Paine scribbled on his drumhead desk during the snowy patriot retreat to the Delaware, "*gives it a superficial appearance of being* RIGHT, *and raises at first a formidable outcry in defense of custom. But the tumult soon subsides.*"

Following the bloodshed on Lexington green, it took 442 days of intense public and private Congressional debate for Paine's "tumult to subside," while the radical revolutionaries voted down every ingenuous conservative compromise and "Olive Branch" appeal to the better nature of George III.

In June 1776 Congress took up the resolution that formally abandoned reconciliation---and made it possible for foreign powers to ally themselves with the new nation. On July 4 it finally declared that "*these United Colonies are, and of Right ought to be, Free and Independent states.*"

Then they told the caretaker at the State House in Philadelphia to go and ring the bell (#627). The Fourth of July has been a favorite American holiday ever since.

#561

He was America's great philosopher-statesman, a scientist, mathematician, and architect---and a skilled politician who hardly ever made a public speech.

In 1779 he wrote an ordinance establishing religious freedom in Virginia. Its clear separation of the powers of church and state is reflected in our Bill of Rights.

From 1779 to 1781 he dodged General Cornwallis's bullets while serving as wartime Governor of Virginia.

In 1784 he wrote a national anti-slavery ordinance---80 years later it helped preserve the Union.

From 1785 to 1789 he was American ambassador to France; following that, U.S. Secretary of State.

In 1797 he became the country's second Vice-President.

In 1801 he became President, and was re-elected four years later. During both terms he battled to preserve a host of newly established democratic ideals.

In 1803, with a stroke of the pen, he doubled the size of the United States, and the following year sent an expedition to the Pacific that ensured our claims to the Northwest.

In 1819 he dreamed into existence one of the world's great universities.

But nothing Thomas Jefferson (#561, 807) ever did compared to the afternoon of June 10, 1776, when, at the age of 33, he sat down in his rented second floor parlor of a German bricklayer's house at the corner of Seventh and Market Streets in Philadelphia, unfolded a portable writing desk made to his own design by a local carpenter, sharpened a quill, pulled the cork from a bottle of ink, took a sheet of imported Dutch paper, and began to write..."*When in the course of human events, it becomes necessary for one people to dissolve the political bands which have connected them with another, and to assume, among the powers of the earth, the separate and equal station to which the laws of nature and of nature's God entitle them...*"

Of all his many remarkable achievements, Jefferson, as he lay dying in 1826, requested only three be carved on his tomb:

> "AUTHOR OF THE DECLARATION OF INDEPENDENCE,
> THE STATUTE OF VIRGINIA FOR RELIGIOUS FREEDOM,
> AND FATHER OF THE UNIVERSITY OF VIRGINIA."

Any *one* would have assured Jefferson eternal glory.

#120

#807

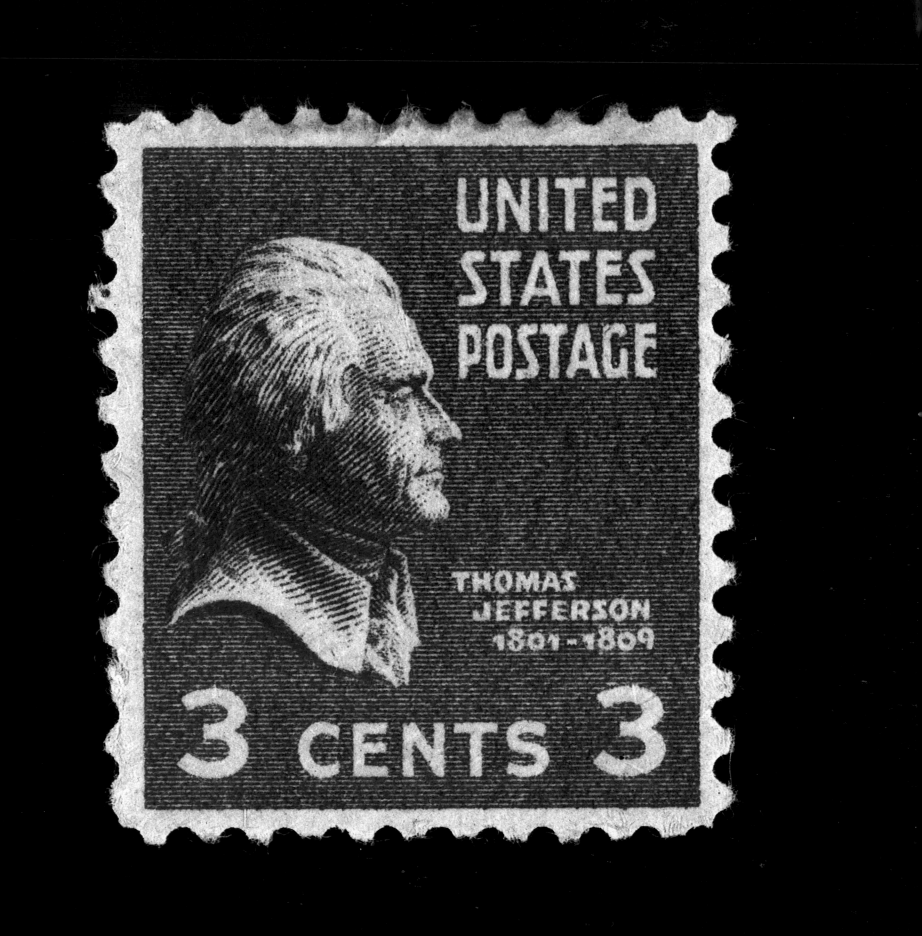

#1003

Espionage for pay is cheap and tawdry, but espionage for a cause can be honorable, even though Secretary of War Henry Stimson once intoned: *"Gentleman do not read other gentlemen's mail."* Even so, George Washington, who was certainly a gentleman, ran one of the most effective spy networks in the history of warfare. In the case of young Nathan Hale, espionage for General Washington's army quickly made him a martyr in the War of Independence.

Born at Coventry, Connecticut, Hale was only 18 when he graduated from Yale in 1773 to become a well-liked schoolteacher. Two years later he marched off to the siege of Boston, and soon received a captain's commission in the Connecticut Rangers, an early Continental commando group.

In September 1776, after the British captured New York City (#1003), Ranger commander Thomas Knowlton called for a volunteer to go behind enemy lines in civilian clothes to spy out the dispositions of General Howe's 22,000-man invasion force. Captain Hale volunteered, rationalizing to a friend: *"Every kind of service that is necessary to the public good becomes honourable by being necessary."*

On the night of September 21, a disastrous fire broke out in the enemy-held city. More than a fifth of New York's homes were destroyed before the wind shifted. Not without cause, the edgy invaders suspected arson, and soon picked up the suspicious-looking young schoolteacher---carrying drawings (with Latin inscriptions) in his pocket. The following morning, in an enemy artillery compound in the middle of Manhattan, without much ado or benefit of clergy, Nathan Hale was hanged from a tree.

As the noose slipped over his neck, history relates that the 21-year-old captain spoke a few brave words: *"I only regret that I have but one life to lose for my country."* Rear Admiral Bartholemew James of the Royal Navy, who watched Hale's execution, noted in his diary how the spy died *"lamenting only that he could not communicate his intelligence to his commander in chief, as he had done with success twice before."*

In the days when a half-cent's worth of postage still had some meaning, the sad fate of this brave young man, whose name has always represented patriotic courage in the face of death, was commemorated on this handsome olive-brown stamp (#551).

British Colonel Henry Hamilton commanded a chain of former French frontier forts and villages stretching almost 500 miles from Detroit to Kaskaskia---in the Ohio and Illinois country above the back part of Virginia. To forestall United States expansion into the upper Mississippi Valley, Hamilton paid native warriors---caught up in a war of others' making---a bounty for every settler's scalp brought to Fort Sackville at Vincennes on the Wabash River. Hamilton was soon called the "*Hair Buyer*."

George Rogers Clark, an aggressive young Virginia frontiersman, determined to put a stop to that practice---and to Colonel Hamilton. In 1778, with a commission from Governor Patrick Henry and the Virginia legislature, Clark took advantage of Hamilton's absence in Detroit to float 600 miles down the Ohio River with 175 back-country volunteers, and seize the British garrisons at Kaskaskia and Cahokia. The French inhabitants were pleased to discover their mother country had by now become an ally of the United States, and gave Clark all the help he needed to capture Vincennes.

The Americans installed a four-man garrison at Fort Sackville, and withdrew to Kaskaskia for the winter. Hamilton immediately swept down from Detroit and retook the fort, making plans to attack Clark at Kaskaskia in the spring.

In midwinter this frontier chess game continued. For 18 days, under the most difficult and exhausting conditions, Clark's drenched and hungry men marched 150 miles in the snow from Kaskaskia back to Vincennes---wading and swimming through breast-high waters of the flooded Illinois countryside, crossing four drowned rivers. Clark's epic journey remains one of the brightest spots of the Revolution.

Re-welcomed by the French villagers at Vincennes, Clark demanded the "Hair Buyer" surrender Fort Sackville. The colonel refused---until, in sight of the fort, the vastly outnumbered besiegers tomahawked several of Hamilton's captured Wabash warriors and threw them in the river. Within hours the American flag flew again over Fort Sackville (#651), and Hamilton was on his way to captivity in Virginia.

With a handful of men, Clark had seized an inland empire that would one day include most of Ohio, Illinois, Indiana, Michigan, and Wisconsin (#795).

#795

DON'T TREAD ON ME

FIRST NAVY JACK 1775

#1354

It's one thing to call out the militia and see them come running. It's another thing to call out the navy---and realize you don't have any. The United States found itself in that predicament on May 25, 1775 when the Second Continental Congress declared war on a country with the greatest naval force afloat.

The British North American fleet numbered 87 warships carrying 6,500 sailors. The 30 enemy men-of-war that were soon sailing in and out of New York harbor carried 824 cannon. That overwhelming naval presence not only monitored every navigable coastal river and estuary, but paralyzed the colonies' waterborne trade, causing major shortages and suffering ashore.

Congress was not idle. It supported the arming of fast merchantmen to prey on British shipping; two-thirds of the American cannon founded during the Revolution went to arm those privateers. The United States also commissioned 11 frigates, built in protected shipyards up and down the coast. It even experimented with a one-man torpedo-carrying submarine.

Esek Hopkins of Rhode Island became the first commander-in-chief of the new Continental Navy (#1354). With a task force of 14 frigates and brigs (mounting 110 guns)--- the entire American fleet---he sailed out of Philadelphia in February 1776 for the first and last American naval campaign of the war. Hopkins was charged with the impossible task of driving the British from Chesapeake Bay and the Carolina coast.

Broadly interpreting his orders, the new commander seized a lot of badly-needed war materiel at Nassau in the Bahamas, then ingloriously retreated home to Newport, Rhode Island, to be bottled up by the British---and censured by Congress.

Sailing out of Philadelphia two months later, John Barry (#790) on the brig *Lexington* became the first Continental naval commander to independently capture a British warship in battle---the Royal Navy's sloop-of-war *Edward*.

One of Hopkins's junior officers, 17th in seniority, was 5' 7" John Paul Jones (#790), who quickly established himself as the shortest and scrappiest fighter in the Continental Navy. In 1779 he carried the Revolution to Britain in his *Bon Homme Richard*, raiding the town of Whitehaven, and winning a legendary victory over *Serapis* in the Channel, less than 200 miles from London. The British called him a pirate.

#645

A nation lives by its myths. Once they appear on stamps, they must be true.

Take Elizabeth Griscom Ross, the upholsterer who entered our historical pantheon only in 1876, thanks to the effective promotion efforts of her grandson, William J. Canby. During the great Philadelphia Centennial Exposition, the little three-story Ross home at 239 Arch Street, exploited by Canby, became an important tourist attraction. Tens of thousands of fairgoers visited the tiny parlor where in June 1776 (according to Canby's presentation) the widowed Betsy sewed together the first American flag, under the personal creative supervision of George Washington *(#1004)*---and showed the Commander-in-chief how to make a five-pointed star with a single snip of the scissors.

Betsy's actual connection with the general was slight; her late husband's uncle was one of Washington's friends. Betsy's grandson conveniently ignored the fact that in June 1776 Washington was 80 miles away, fortifying New York City.

Like the tale of the cherry tree; the silver dollar flung across the Rappahannock; and George Washington's unquestioned ability to sleep in almost every farmhouse on the East Coast; Americans quickly accepted the likeable Betsy Ross story.

An even more moving Washington tribute was provided by Mason Locke Weems, author of the *Drunkard's Looking Glass* and other "improving tracts." Weems was the same parson who invented the cherry tree myth in the fifth (1800) edition of his *"Life of George Washington, with Curious Anecdotes Equally Honorable to Himself and Exemplary to his Young Countrymen."*

In *The Federalist* for 1804, Weems developed the new tale of a pious Valley Forge Quaker, tory Isaac Potts, who happened upon Washington at prayer in 1778. Weems's invention was so well received that he incorporated it into the eighth edition of his little biography. The graphic description of Washington down on his knees in the snow, with Potts spying from behind a leafless tree, has inspired countless paintings and lithographs. It has even graced a 1928 postage stamp *(#645)* celebrating the sesquicentennial of the Valley Forge encampment. The image of the General at prayer appeared again for Christmas 1977.

Like Halley's comet, Washington on his knees in the snow will probably return to us with regularity.

#1004

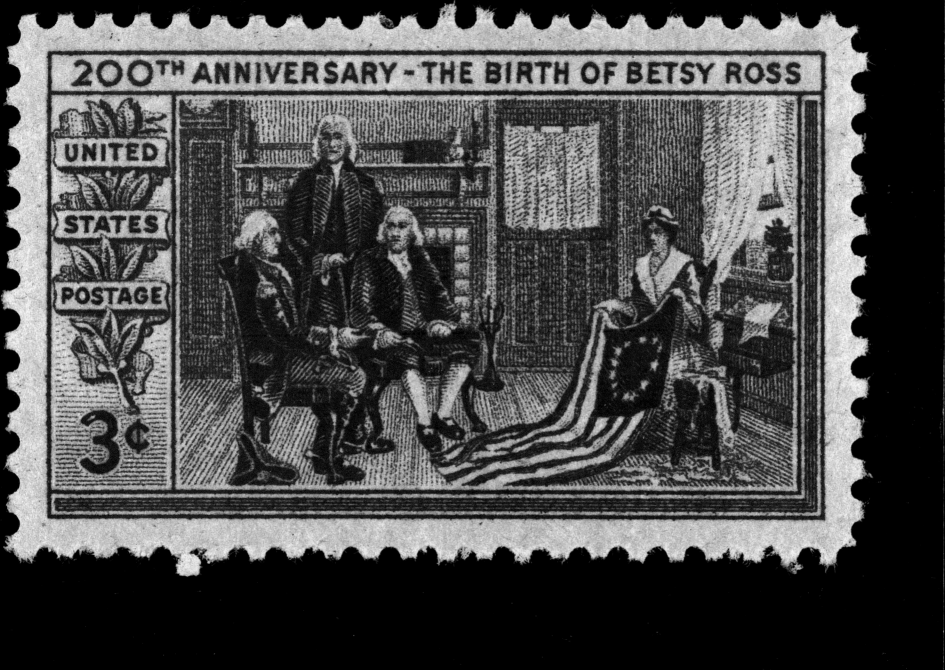

#643

By June 1776, France was secretly shipping supplies to the Continental Army; the following summer it was ready to declare war on Great Britain. The only thing lacking was some reasonable signal that Louis XVI would not be backing a losing cause. That signal, ironically, came from a flamboyant British general named John Burgoyne.

In July 1777, "Gentleman Johnny" set forth from Montreal for Albany with a grand army of 7,173 troops. Less than three months and 180 miles later, he surrendered the whole kit and kaboodle to General Horatio Gates at Saratoga (#644)---not including 896 Hessians previously lost to the Green Mountain Boys (#643) on a horse-stealing raid into western Vermont.

What caused Burgoyne's disaster? History has often gossiped about missing military orders mysteriously pigeonholed at the British War Office, orders supposedly bringing General Howe's army back from Philadelphia and sending it up the Hudson River to aid Burgoyne. But who needed lost orders when Burgoyne, an amateur poet and playwright, was always ready to shoot himself in the foot?

George Bernard Shaw's *The Devil's Disciple* (the only truly interesting play ever written about the American Revolution) casts Burgoyne as a witty and urbane intellectual; actually he was a mean-spirited braggart. At home they called him "*Il Pomposo*."

Burgoyne was in his element when he launched his campaign from Canada. He penned a proclamation to the rebellious citizens of New York and New England, calling himself a "*Messenger of Justice and of Wrath*." He warned of the "*Devastation, Famine, and every concomitant Horror that a reluctant but indispensable Prosecution of Military Duty must occasion.*"

The American response was predictable. Once their crops were in, militiamen from all over western New England and eastern New York came flocking to join Gates's Continentals. In a series of bloody battles, the Americans successfully blocked the road to Albany, surrounded Burgoyne at Saratoga, and compelled his surrender (#644).

It was one of the Decisive Battles of the World. Less than two months later, French foreign office representatives advised the American envoys in Paris that Louis XVI was now ready to sign a formal alliance with the United States .

#644

#734

Inspired by the high-minded ideals of the Declaration of Independence, a sizeable group of foreign volunteers descended on the Continental Army.

Four officers stood out, offering special skills to the infant republic. One lost his life in a gallant, foolhardy cavalry charge.

❧

Tadeusz Andrzej Bonawentura Kosciuszko (#734) was a 30-year-old Polish captain of artillery when he entered the service of the United States. He had studied military science in France. At a time when skilled army engineers were at a premium, Kosciuszko quickly distinguished himself. He was given a colonel's rank, and Washington made him his adjutant. Replacing a temperamental French engineer at West Point, he swiftly turned that raw post into an impregnable bastion.

Kosciuszko's charm soon made him one of the most popular officers in the Continental Army. He had served with great distinction at Saratoga, where he fortified strategic Bemis Heights. Four years later he helped lay out the Yorktown siege lines that choked Cornwallis.

At the close of the war, Congress acknowledged Kosciuszko's devoted service by making him a citizen, granting him land and a pension, and naming him a brigadier general. Returning to Poland, Kosciuszko retained that military title in his native country's struggle for its own political independence.

❧

Casimir Pulaski (#690), a Polish count, was a quarrelsome 29-year-old dragoon in exile from his native land. In the summer of 1777, armed with a letter of recommendation from Benjamin Franklin, he was accepted as a Continental cavalry officer. Pulaski saw spirited action at Brandywine and Germantown, and Congress put him in charge of four new dragoon regiments, naming him a brigadier general and "Commander of the Horse."

Two years later, when he petulantly chose not to serve under Anthony Wayne, Pulaski was ordered to the southern theater, where he raised a mixed corps known as *Pulaski's Legion*. The unit was badly beaten during the defense of Charleston in May 1779. Five months later Pulaski received a bit of grapeshot in the groin while leading a cavalry charge during the joint Franco-American attack on Savannah. In two days he was dead.

#690

If the Revolution spawned a rising star, it was Marie Joseph Paul Yves Roch Gilbert du Motier, marquis de Lafayette (#1010). Only 20 years old, this titled orphan, speaking almost no English, slipped away from a French cavalry captaincy, ducked a restraining order from Louis XVI, and sailed to serve under Washington, who soon became his lifelong friend. *"At the first news of your quarrel,"* Lafayette told him, *"my heart was enrolled in it."*

#1010

Congress was so impressed with his character, lineage, and wealth that they took Franklin's advice and made Lafayette a major general, to serve at his own expense. Despite what Jefferson once called Lafayette's "canine appetite for popularity and fame," he never gave the legislators cause for regret.

Lafayette made signal contributions to the success of the French Alliance. He distinguished himself in the field, particularly as a cavalry commander harassing Cornwallis's retreat to Yorktown. After the war he returned to France, and became involved in the revolutionary events that subsequently rocked his native country and the rest of Europe.

In 1824, at the invitation of President Monroe, Lafayette returned for a triumphal tour of the 48-year-old United States.

❦

Frederick William August Heinrich Ferdinand, Baron von Steuben (#689), was a Prussian officer who fought in the Seven Years' War and served briefly as an aide-de-camp to Frederick the Great. Having lost favor at court, von Steuben was at loose ends in Paris in 1777 when he met Ben Franklin. The American envoy astutely recognized the value of von Steuben's Prussian general-staff training, and wrote a letter to Congress introducing him as a "Lieutenant General" willing to serve without pay.

At Valley Forge, the 48-year-old drillmaster, unable to speak English, was still able to teach the inexperienced American soldiers his own modified version of the Prussian military drill. He achieved what has been called "the most rapid military training course in the history of the world." Within two months Congress made him inspector general of the army.

#689

Von Steuben's *Regulations for the Order and Discipline of the Troops of the United States* remained the army drill manual for 33 years. After the war four states gave von Steuben land; Congress honored him with a gold-hilted sword, and a substantial pension.

"The late affair has almost broke my heart," wrote Charles Earl Cornwallis on January 21, 1781. He was bemoaning the American victory over his army's left wing four days earlier at Cowpens, South Carolina---329 British casualties, 600 taken prisoner. The two-hour battle also put a dent in the military reputation of Cornwallis's 27-year-old *wunderkind* cavalryman, Lieutenant Colonel Banastre Tarleton, who fled the field.

Cornwallis's concern was prophetic. Nine months later, after a pyrrhic will-o'-the-wisp campaign through the Carolinas and Virginia, his entire Southern command was trapped at the tip of the York Peninsula.

In a striking example of elaborate international, interservice cooperation---following a year of inactivity at Newport---General Jean Baptiste Donatien de Vimeur, comte de Rochambeau (#703) and his 4,000 French troops marched and sailed with 9,500 of Washington's (#703) Continentals 450 miles to Yorktown, where Lafayette and von Steuben had succeeded in bottling up Cornwallis.

The allied forces also kept a planned rendezvous with 34 French warships under Francois Joseph Paul, comte de Grasse (#703), who sailed up from the West Indies. De Grasse blockaded the York and James Rivers, drove off a British reinforcement fleet from New York, and sent an additional 3,800 French troops ashore.

The classic siege of Yorktown, one of the great battles of the 18th century, commenced October 6, 1781. When someone asked patriot Governor Thomas Nelson of Virginia where they should aim the first cannon shot, he unselfishly pointed to his own captured home. Days and nights were filled with incessant digging, crashing explosives, and mad combat.

After 11 days of mounting British casualties, a redcoated drummer boy climbed atop a crumbling enemy parapet and beat for parley; his rataplan went almost unheard amidst all the noise. Cornwallis asked for 24 hours to work out terms; Washington gave him two. At the surrender field on October 20, a British military band played *The World Turned Upside Down*.

Ten days later a second British relief fleet arrived from New York. *"Too late,"* quipped a French officer, *"the chicken is already eaten."*

#552

Ben Franklin (*#24, 552*) was the person who comes along once in the history of a country---*if it is lucky*. From the humblest of beginnings, Ben grew up to be a witty, wise, and winning man, respected on both sides of the Atlantic for his statemanship and practical philosophy. In *Poor Richard's Almanack*, he encouraged reasonable concepts of prudence, common sense, and honesty, embodying his ideas in timeless aphorisms everybody can recite.

Franklin's life spanned three tumultuous, historic eras. Born in Boston less than 100 years after the Pilgrims landed at Plimouth, he lived through the Revolution to see George Washington inaugurated as President of the United States. His optimistic 84 seasons were characterized by an *"indelible affection for my dear Country."*

In quick succession, Franklin was, among other things, a soap boiler, candlemaker, ballad hawker, printer, essayist, drygoods clerk, newspaperman, almanac publisher, linguist, insurance broker, inventor, Indian agent, experimenter, scientist, military contractor, revolutionist, diplomat, international peace negotiator---and of course, the first Postmaster General of the United States.

To list everything Franklin did for British North America, the War of Independence, the infant United States---and the world---would take volumes far larger than this. His own modest *Autobiography* recounts only his earliest years---yet runs to more than 70,000 words.

Near the end of Franklin's tireless public life, he agreed to lend his considerable political prestige to the Constitutional Convention in Philadelphia, serving as its oldest and most patient delegate.

After suggesting key compromises that would allow a majority of Founding Fathers to sign their names to the document that has since guided our lives, Franklin pointed to a carved and gilded sun on the back of the President's chair.

He turned to the other delegates and said: *"Painters have always found it hard to show the difference between a rising and a setting sun. How many times during this difficult assembly have I looked at that American sun and wondered---is it rising...or setting? This day I finally have the happiness to know. Our sun is* RISING*."*

What a man!

#803

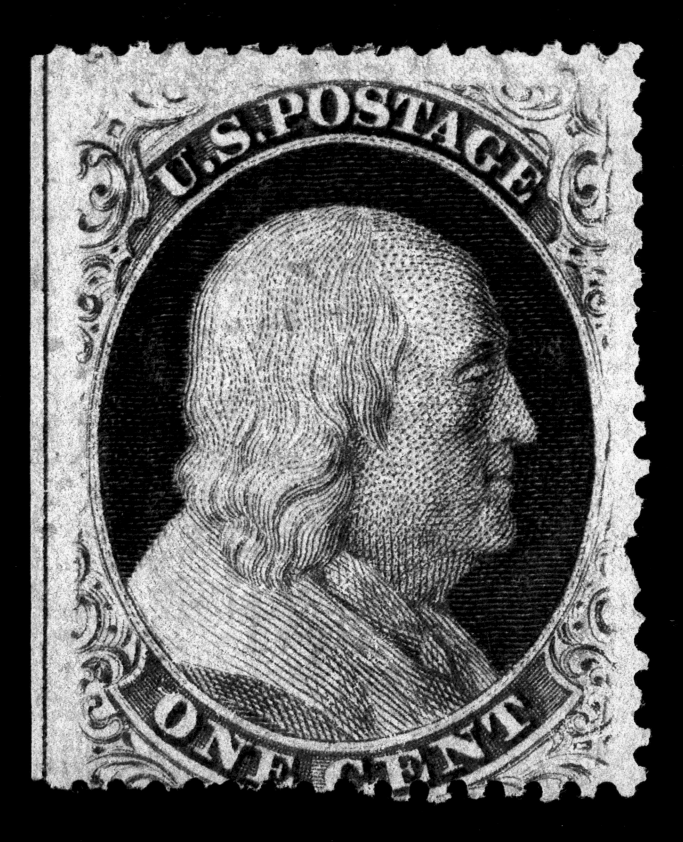

"THIS IS THE PLACE"

1847 THE UTAH CENT

THE EARLY EXPANSIONISTS

#798

On May 14, 1787, a meeting was called in Philadelphia's State House (#798) *"for the express and sole purpose of revising the Articles of Confederation."* Its true purpose was hidden; it was actually a convention to draft a new United States constitution. A half century later President van Buren accurately described that Philadelphia gathering as "an heroic and lawless act."

On June 1, when discussion among the 55 delegates from 12 states reached Number 7 of Virginia's basic Resolves: *"that a national executive be instituted,"* the meeting fell strangely silent. Washington left the chair and maintained an austere silence. It was a foregone conclusion that the former Commander-in-chief would be a major figure in any new government; James Madison found the ongoing debate in Washington's presence "peculiarly embarrassing."

Of all the problems facing the drafters of this unauthorized new charter of American government, the question of a single or multiple executive was one of the thorniest. George III's name was never mentioned, but everyone present had played some role in the desperate struggle to rid the colonies of *that* single---and single-minded---chief executive.

Then came the violent pros and cons. *Vigor, dispatch,* and *responsibility,* argued one delegate, were best found in a single man. Such attributes, answered another, would also be found in three men; he called a sole executive a *"fetus for monarchy."* A plural executive, countered a third delegate, would be too easily swayed by sectional interests.

How would an overly ambitious single executive be controlled? Should he serve four years? Seven? Life? Franklin sided with the pluralists: "The first man we put at the helm will be a good one. Nobody knows what may come afterwards."

In the end the states voted seven to three for a single executive: *"Article. II. Section. 1. The executive Power shall be vested in a President..."* Madison recorded Virginia's vote, with "GEN. W.... AYE."

Six hundred and ninety-nine days later, on the balcony of the Federal Building on Wall Street in New York City, George Washington took the oath of office as the first (and sole) chief executive of the United States (#854).

He was our first and last universally loved president.

#854

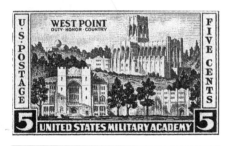

#789

Credit for the idea of a government academy to educate and train young Americans for military service goes to General Henry Knox, in 1776. The concept was reinvigorated seven years later by Brigadier General Jedediah Huntington, commanding at West Point, the army fortress on the Hudson called "the Key to the United States." Huntington suggested to George Washington that "an Academy might here be instituted for instruction in all the branches of the Military Art."

It took two decades for Congress, with prodding from Washington and Alexander Hamilton, to authorize establishment of the United States Military Academy---since known informally as *"West Point."* The Academy admitted its first small group of young engineering cadets in 1802. In its earliest days it suffered from laxity and disorganization, but the War of 1812 underlined the country's need for better-trained army officers, and the *"Point"* took on new importance.

Beginning in 1817 under the 16-year superintendency of Major Sylvanus Thayer---an early graduate, subsequently known as the "father of the Military Academy"---West Point reorganized and broadened its original engineering curriculum to include a wide range of college-level instruction. Since the days of Thayer, the Academy has graduated tens of thousands of disciplined cadets as junior commissioned officers in the United States Army. Many have gone on to become distinguished figures in U.S. military history.

From a few wooden barracks on the parade ground behind Fort Clinton, the United States Military Academy has slowly spread over many acres, with an imposing array of gothic granite structures containing dormitories, teaching facilities, libraries, and administrative offices (#789).

Forty-three years after the establishment of the Military Academy, Navy Secretary George Bancroft (also a historian and educator) became dissatisfied with the methods of training midshipmen. In 1845 he established a facility to train junior naval officers---the "Naval School at Annapolis" (#794). During the Civil War the Academy moved to Newport, Rhode Island, but returned to Maryland in 1865. It has grown into a huge educational complex on the shores of Chesapeake Bay (#984).

#984

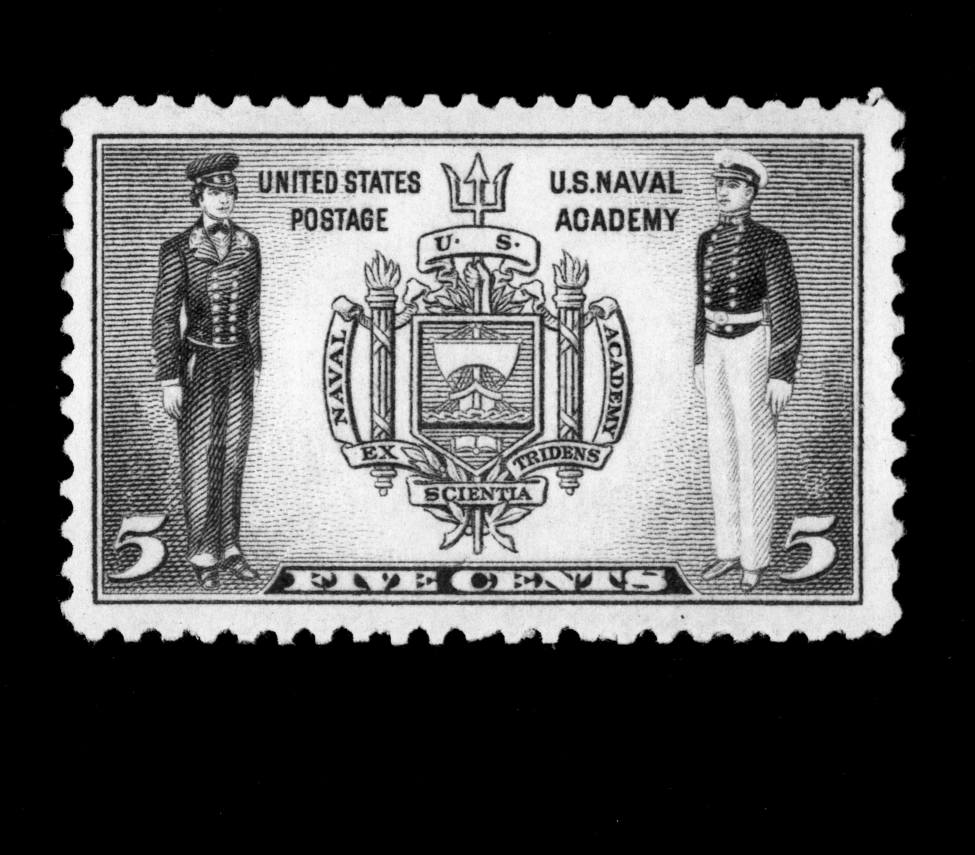

#1053

If Alexander Hamilton (#1053) hadn't insisted that the federal government assume state debts, and Thomas Jefferson hadn't wished to see our new capital established below the Mason-Dixon Line, the *White House* and *Capitol* might today be in Trenton. Or in Philadelphia. Or in Baltimore, Lancaster, York, Princeton, Annapolis, or New York. From 1774 to 1789, all those cities served at one time or another as the capital of our new nation.

But Hamilton and Jefferson successfully effected their political horse-trade. In 1790 the Congressional followers of those two arch-enemies followed the Constitutional mandate to pick a new "*Seat of Government of the United States*" (Article I, Section 8). They chose a "*District (not exceeding ten Miles square)*" lying on the banks of the Potomac River above its confluence with the Anacostia.

Under President Washington's direction, three commissioners defined and surveyed that new "*Territory of Columbia.*" They purchased or accepted the necessary land from Maryland, Virginia, and private owners, and provided for construction of suitable buildings for the public offices of the United States---all to be ready by the first Monday in December 1800. We became the first nation in the world to erect our seat of government from scratch.

The president chose Revolutionary War veteran Pierre L'Enfant to plan the new "*Federal City,*" with Benjamin Banneker, an African-American architect, and Andrew Ellicott, a Virginia surveyor, to help lay it out. The 36-year-old French engineer planned rectangular blocks cut by major diagonal avenues, neatly converging at the Houses of Congress and the executive mansion. The unusual grid created scores of squares, circles, and triangles---perfect, thought L'Enfant, for lots of monuments and statues. He has not been disappointed.

Construction of the White House (#990) began in 1792; the Capitol (#572), a year later. "*We shall soon have a city,*" George Washington announced, "*though not as large as London, yet with a magnitude not inferior to few others in Europe.*" In 1800 the federal government, led by President Thomas Jefferson, began moving into its new home on the Potomac.

Thirteen years later the British burned it down, and we had to start all over again.

#990

#1063

By March 1803, the admission of four additional states had added more than 130,000 square miles to the new Federal Union. But nothing in *Article IV, Section 3* of the 14-year-old United States Constitution remotely suggested any way to handle Napoleon Bonaparte's unexpected offer to Thomas Jefferson.

The new ruler of France, teetering on the edge of a devastating war with Great Britain, surprised U.S. envoys Robert R. Livingston and James Monroe with a bid to sell us 827,192 square miles of French-held land in west-central North America, east of the Rockies *(#327)*.

The territory was almost four times the size of France. It included the key port of New Orleans (secretly conveyed to Napoleon by Spain in 1800) plus the huge area the early French explorers of the western Mississippi basin had christened "Louisiana" after their king.

"The future destinies of our country hang on the event of this negotiation," Jefferson wrote anxiously to his ambassadors in Paris. With one stroke of his pen, for only $15 million in bonds and liquidated U.S. damages against French naval depredations, this otherwise "strict constructionist" President embraced the theory of "implied Constitutional powers" and took Napoleon's offer.

For less than 35¢ an acre, Jefferson peacefully doubled the size of the United States, adding what would one day become Arkansas, Iowa, Louisiana, Missouri, Nebraska, North Dakota, Oklahoma, South Dakota, and parts of Colorado, Kansas, Minnesota, Montana, and Wyoming.

Like a kid in a candy store, Jefferson itched to discover exactly what he had bought. Within half a year, he authorized a well-organized military and scientific expedition, led by his private secretary, Captain Meriwether Lewis, and George Rogers Clark's younger brother William *(#1063)*.

The little group left St. Louis May 14, 1804, returning 832 days later. During those two years Lewis and Clark, with the help of a Shoshone native American woman as guide and interpreter, traveled vast distances to the far-off "Oregon country" and return---a trip equal to almost one-fifth of the way around the world. The expedition established our irrevocable claim to the Pacific Northwest.

The effect on U.S. westward expansion was incalculable.

#327

#951

UNITED STATES
3¢

1797 U·S· FRIGATE

#229

If it wasn't for Dr. William Beames of Upper Marlborough, Maryland, we'd probably all be singing *America the Beautiful* (with music from a Samuel Ward hymn) at the start of every ball game.

Dr. Beames was arrested for interfering with a British shore party during the War of 1812. He was taken aboard one of Admiral Sir George Cockburn's warships, outside Baltimore harbor. The doctor's best friend, a 35-year-old Fredericktown lawyer named Francis Scott Key (#962), volunteered to visit the admiral's flagship, *H.M.S. Surprise*, under a flag of truce. On September 13, 1814, Key was able to successfully negotiate Beames's release.

At that moment, however, the entire British fleet began a heavy bombardment of Baltimore's Fort McHenry. When Key came on deck the next morning, the little fort guarding the port's inner harbor was still there---with its red, white and blue flag still flying triumphantly.

Key grabbed a pencil and composed four stanzas of a patriotic song he called *The Bombardment of Fort McHenry*. For musical accompaniment, the young attorney chose *To Anacreon in Heaven*, not a hymn but a hard-to-sing English tippling song popular on both sides of the Atlantic.

For a person of average vocal range, what we now call *The Star-Spangled Banner* is no picnic, but everyone usually tries to do his or her best.

Andrew Jackson's lopsided victory at New Orleans, plus Oliver Hazard Perry's (*#229*) stirring success on Lake Erie ("*Don't Give Up the Ship!*") usually tend to obscure general British nastiness during the War of 1812; singers usually slip by Key's vigorous third verse:

> *And where is the band who so vauntingly swore*
> *That the havoc of war and the battle's confusion*
> *A home and a country would leave us no more?*
> *Their blood has washed out their foul footsteps' pollution.*
> *No refuge could save the hireling and slave*
> *From the terror of flight or the gloom of the grave!*

In 1931, President Hoover and Congress made Key's song our national anthem. We've been singing it in public (skipping that third verse) ever since.

#962

#783

1836 OREGON

PACIFIC OCEAN

WASHINGTON

COLUMBIA RIVER

ASTORIA

OREGON

WALLA WALLA

OREGON

125 121

49

47

45

43

121

3

U.S. POSTAGE

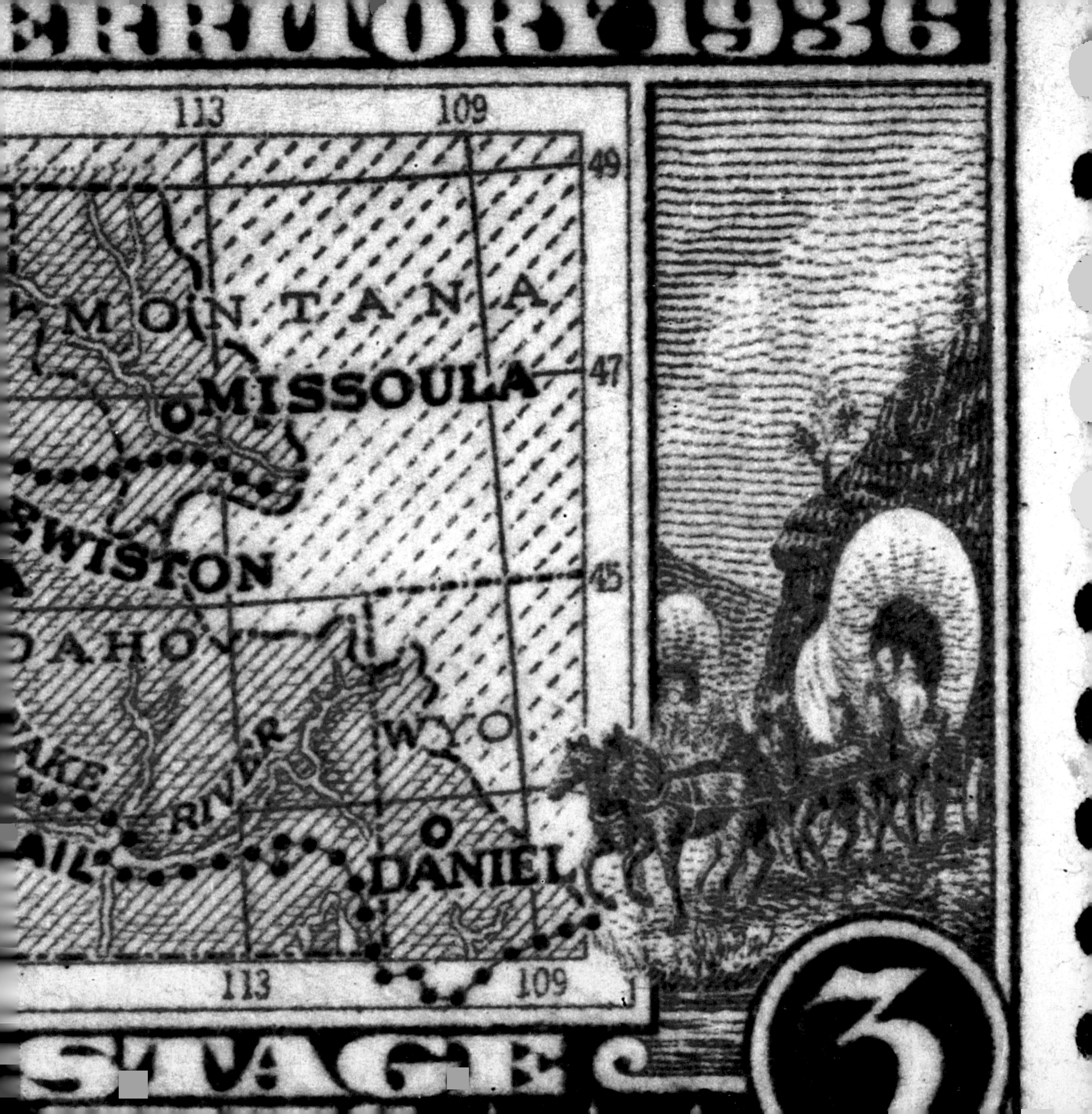

113 109

49

MONTANA

oMISSOULA 47

EWISTON 45

DAHO

RIVER WYO.

AKE

AIL

O
DANIEL

113 109

3

Following Mexico's war of independence from Spain in the 1820s, many southern farmers crossed from Louisiana into the sparsely populated area of northeastern Mexico called *Texas*. They were seeking inexpensive land on which to raise cotton. Those with African-American slaves brought them along.

The Mexican government turned down every United States offer to buy the area, but continued to encourage immigration. Lured by promises of separate Mexican statehood, entrepreneur/politicians like Stephen Fuller Austin (#776) obtained large land grants and established flourishing American colonies. Soon there were more than 20,000 Americans in Texas; ten per cent were slaves.

In 1830, the Mexican government suddenly changed course, barring further immigration, or importation of slaves, and established steep customs duties enforced by the military. It was six years before Texans felt ready to challenge General Antonio López de Santa Anna, a revolutionary hero who had seized political power as "ultimate dictator." Ostensibly acting in defense of the usurped Mexican constitution, Texans declared their independence.

Santa Anna marched north, won a few minor skirmishes, and overwhelmed 180 Texans (including Jim Bowie and Davy Crockett) who fought to the death in a fortified Franciscan mission called *The Alamo* (#776). Thousands of volunteers soon rallied behind Sam Houston (#776) and captured Santa Anna; Texas became independent.

After nine years of political maneuvering, the slaveholding Texans beat back the abolitionist forces in Congress, and in 1845 the United States finally annexed the Republic of Texas. An all-out invasion of Mexico soon followed, during and after which the United States acquired a vast western/southwestern empire, eventually divided up into all or parts of ten states.

Eighteen hundred miles away in a Massachusetts jail, Henry David Thoreau explained to friends why he was not paying his "Mexican War tax." *"If I have unjustly wrested a plank from a drowning man,"* wrote the pencil-maker from Concord, *"I must restore it to him, though I drown myself. This people must cease to make war on Mexico."*

Thoreau's voice was a lonely one.

#562

During its early years, a relatively weak United States edged cautiously through the minefield of European great-power politics. American leaders were often forced to improvise reactions to overseas provocations. From such expedient and often contradictory responses emerged major principles of American foreign policy.

For example, the columns of Claypoole's Philadelphia *American Daily Advertiser* for September 19, 1796, carried a warning to readers to eschew foreign alliances, but always maintain "*a respectably defensive posture*." The words were George Washington's, from his (never orally delivered) *Farewell Address*.

Eighteen years later, serving both as Madison's Secretary of State and Secretary of War, James Monroe (#562) had occasion to reflect on such "respectably defensive postures" while fleeing a British army detachment on its way to burn the White House.

During his second term as President of the United States, Monroe, now at peace with the British, faced a new problem: Western Hemisphere destablization caused by Spanish attempts to suppress Latin American revolutionaries.

The President used his annual message to Congress in 1824 to enunciate a bold new principle of resistance to European intervention in the political affairs of the Western Hemisphere, a *Doctrine* that remains a cornerstone of American foreign policy.

Monroe presided over the end of an unusual "Era of Good Feelings." Two administrations later, Andrew Jackson (#73p) was elected by the voters of the 24 states to lead a different kind of country, one that had become more politically and economically fragmented than the founding fathers ever dreamed possible.

Jackson's immense appeal came from his record as an 1812 war hero, following his youth on the log cabin frontier. Resisting intimidation by Congressional sectionalists, he used his veto unsparingly. Jackson also cautioned against slavish reliance on the infallibility of the Supreme Court---stressing the "*great advantage and propriety of the judgment of the people*."

His civil service reforms, denounced by critics as a "spoils system," were merely Jackson's attempt (he said) to eject office-holders who had developed a "*habit of looking with indifference upon the public interest*."

It was a fresh age for American politics.

#1120

Every American knows about the Pony Express. Not everyone realizes the expressmen rode horses, not ponies---and that this unique western mail delivery service ended almost as soon as it began.

Even so, the image of those 19th century Pony Express riders (#894) still remains fresh and vivid. We all grew up with colorful stories of those intrepid young men, battling their way though every kind of western weather, galloping in and out of 150 relay stations that stretched across half the North American continent.

The Express riders were tough. They had to be to cover up to 75 miles on each shift, before passing on the mail pouch to the next horseman. They swapped mounts on the fly, forded rushing rivers, hurtled through difficult mountain passes, crossed barren deserts, and even outran "enemy hostiles"---just to move a small bag of important letters and telegrams from Missouri to California in eight days.

What a vast improvement the Pony Express was over the old Butterfield Stage Line (*#1120*), whose longer southern route took three weeks!

The Pony Express---more properly the "Overland Mail Delivery Service"---was spurred into existence at the first rumblings of civil war. It was put together by Alexander Majors of Kentucky, whose government contract specified the fastest possible exchange of important political and business communications between the established states and distant California (#997).

Messages were first carried for $5 an ounce. As the popularity of the service grew, the cost dropped to $1. The legendary connection lasted only 18 months, long enough for telegraph wires to be strung from St. Joseph, Missouri, over the Rockies and Sierras, all the way to Sacramento. After October 24, 1861, the horses and riders were slowly phased out.

The fastest trip was made in 7 days 17 hours from the St. Joseph telegraph office to Placerville, California---March 4 to March 11, 1861. The riders carried Abraham Lincoln's 3,500-word First Inaugural Address 2,000 miles through the wilderness---proof to everyone on the West Coast that (in the President's own words) *"The Union of these States is perpetual."*

#894

#1061

#997, #

1954

#114

In 1829, the first railroading mistake made in America was to order a British locomotive too heavy for U.S. tracks. It inspired Matthias Baldwin to build the first domestic locomotive---*Old Ironsides*---for the Philadelphia, Germantown, and Norristown Railroad. Soon the Baldwin Works held the lion's share of the American locomotive business. One of its early engines is shown on this 1869 pictorial stamp (*#114*).

Railroading became America's growth industry. By 1850, rails tied the Atlantic coast to the Great Lakes; three years later, to Chicago; three years after that to the west bank of the Mississippi River.

But the greatest challenge still lay ahead. In the midst of civil war, Congress decided that a rail line across the continent would strengthen the military, political, and economic ties that bound the Union. Where a Pony Express rider and telegraph wire could go (the legislators reasoned), so could steel rails.

In 1862, Congress authorized two separate companies to construct a transcontinental railroad line between Omaha, Nebraska, and Sacramento, California. To ease future connections, the government mandated a 4' 8-1/2" track width. That gauge soon became standard for all major American railroads.

For every mile of track laid, each company received a gift of 20 alternating sections of public land, plus subsidies of $16,000 for level construction, $32,000 for work in the hills, and $48,000 for blasting through mountain passes. When construction dragged, Congress doubled the land grant (finally totaling *33 million acres*), improved other terms, and allowed the companies to solicit private capital. The great Stanford, Crocker, Huntington, and Hopkins railroad fortunes were on their way.

After four years of difficult construction, the Union Pacific Railroad (building westward through the Rockies with Irish immigrants), and the Central Pacific Railroad (building eastward through the Sierras with Chinese immigrants), joined tracks May 10, 1869, at Promontory Point, Utah (*#922*). To celebrate the great day, a golden rail spike was driven into the last tie with a silver sledgehammer.

By some patriotic accident of geography, America's newest railroad line was exactly 1,776 miles long.

#922

LINCOLN

THE SECTIONALISTS

#555

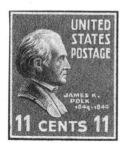

#816

On December 22, 1847, 19 days after arriving from Springfield, Illinois, Abraham Lincoln (#1113) stood up in the 30th U.S. Congress and delivered his maiden speech. It was a slightly sarcastic series of resolutions attacking government conduct in connection with the Mexican War.

Three months earlier American troops had captured Mexico City. The 38-year-old Whig from Illinois presented eight resolutions drawn up to embarrass administration Democrats attempting to negotiate a Draconian peace treaty with Mexico. In a tone not dissimilar to Thoreau's *Essay on Civil Disobedience*, the resolutions suggested that President James K. Polk (#816) had maneuvered a pliable government into an illegitimate conflict.

Although no one in the House of Representatives, including Lincoln, was ready to say so, the negotiations that eventually led to the Treaty of Guadalupe Hidalgo were ultimately concerned with the dreaded "S" word; the treaty-makers anticipated further extension of African-American slavery. As arid midwestern and western territories with short growing seasons were slowly carved up into new pieces of the United States, President Polk was unwilling to see slavery trapped within such rigorous geographical boundaries.

Citing Polk's bellicose claims before the previous Congress, Lincoln's "*Spot Resolutions*" demanded details on the specific American *spots* where previous to the May 13, 1846, U.S. declaration of war, Mexican troops had "invaded our soil in hostile array," and allegedly "shed the blood of *our citizens.*"

Were not those "*citizens,*" Lincoln demanded, actually "armed *officers* and *soldiers*" sent *across* the Mexican border "by the military order of the President?" In 600 words, the gangling Illinois freshman Representative demonstrated how the President of the United States had misled the American people.

The House tabled Lincoln's resolutions, the punitive peace negotiations continued, and even Lincoln's own constituency refused him support. But national politicians took notice of this bold young country lawyer, with glints of unusual courage under a homespun frontier exterior.

The next time Mr. Lincoln went to Washington, 14 years and several hundred speeches later (#1115), it was to be sworn in as the sixteenth President of the United States.

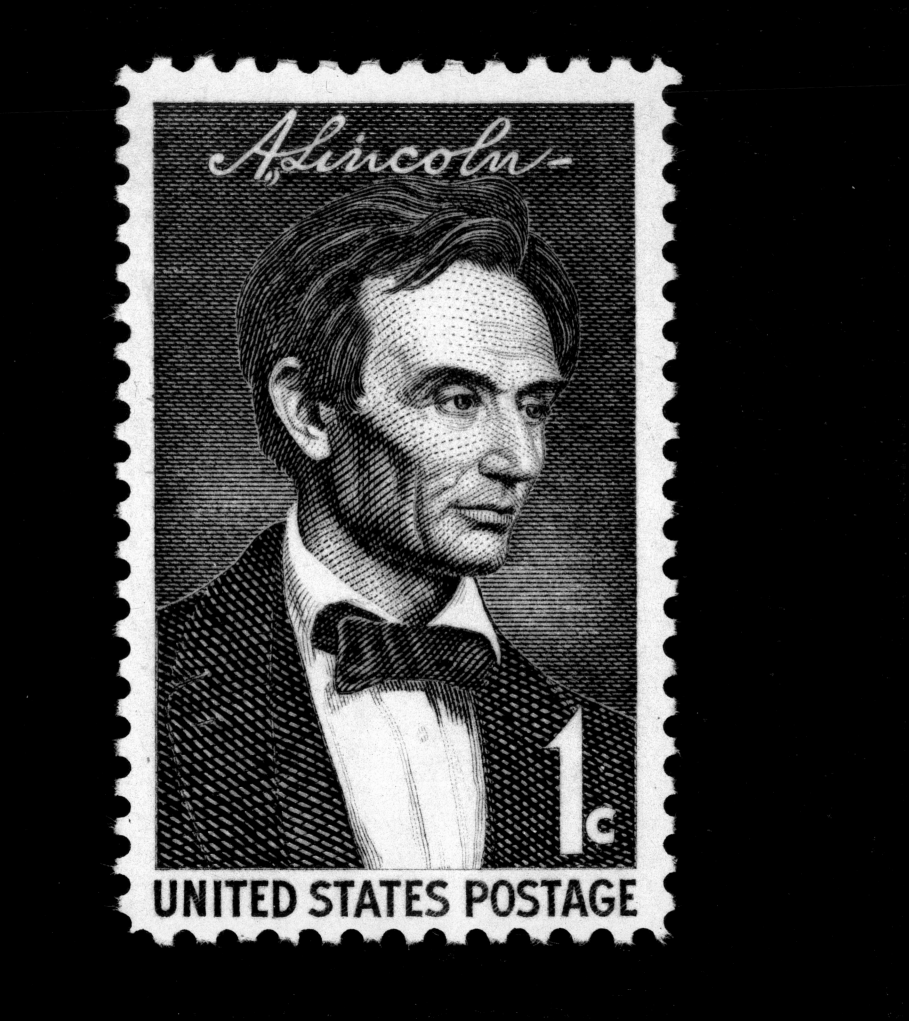

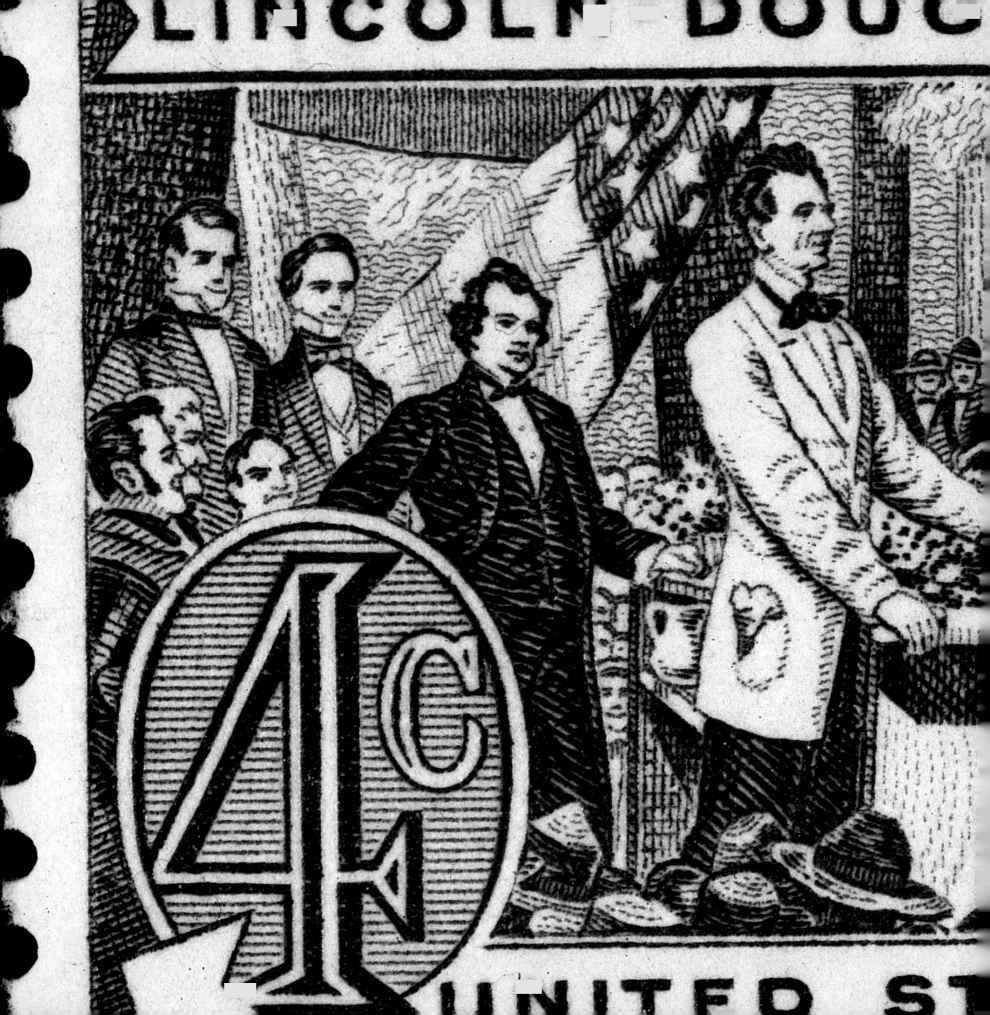

4c

#725

As the 18 northern and 14 southern states maintained a collision course over the expansion of African-American slavery in the western United States, and endless Congressional debate continued over the binding nature of the federal compact, political compromise seemed the only way to keep the country from splitting apart.

Outnumbered in the House of Representatives, the slave states still wielded power in the Senate. Many were prepared to abandon the 70-year-old republic. Only a handful of Northern and Southern leaders had sufficient prestige to avert disaster.

In 1849, after a long and distinguished political career, 73-year-old Henry Clay of Virginia (#309) returned to the Senate to help defuse the controversy over whether slavery should be legally barred from territories ceded by Mexico.

Two years earlier, Representative David Wilmot of Pennsylvania had tacked an amendment onto the appropriations bill supplying President Polk with $2 million to negotiate the final peace treaty with the Mexicans. Wilmot's amendment barred slavery from any newly acquired territories. For two years in a row the House passed the amended bill; for two years the Senate refused to consider it. The violent argument crystallized increasing sectional bitterness.

Clay's patchwork solution was a package of conciliatory resolutions known as the "Compromise of 1850." Passed after memorable Congressional debate, the legislation succeeded in trading a more stringent fugitive slave law for admission of California as a free state; prohibited the slave trade (but not slavery) in the District of Columbia; established the Territories of New Mexico and Utah (#950) without mentioning slavery (the problem could be negotiated later); and settled Texas's claims on New Mexico with a payment of $10 million.

Sixty-eight-year-old Senator Daniel Webster of Massachusetts (#725), a lifelong abolitionist, nevertheless insisted that the union of the states be preserved at any cost. Supporting Clay's compromise, Webster delivered an eloquent speech whose conclusion, "*Liberty and Union, now and forever, one and inseparable*," quickly entered the elocution books.

Webster's 40 years of political influence assured the success of the unwieldy compromise. The Civil War was postponed.

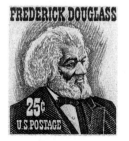

#1290

By the mid-19th century, more words had been written and spoken about the institution of African-American slavery than any other social and political aspect of United States history.

It was a time of unparalleled dissidence. While abolitionists stormed against the working conditions of southern plantation labor, and risked jail and even death to rescue fugitive slaves from their legal masters, generations of educated slaveholders quoted the Bible and even Greek philosophers to justify the "expediency and rightness" of exploiting slave labor.

But slaveholding in antiquity was always accompanied by some recognition of human and family values, often with conditions that eventually led to manumission. In the southern United States, this was rarely the case. The infamous slave ships that carried Africans to bondage in this country set a depersonalized tone whose vestiges still trouble the relationship between American whites and blacks.

From the times of Sojourner Truth, Harriet Tubman, and Frederick Douglass (*#1290*), to those of Martin Luther King (*#1771*), many African-Americans, including hundreds of Revolutionary and thousands of Civil War soldiers, played a major role in bringing people of color *Up from Slavery*---to use the title of Booker Taliaferro Washington's (*#873*) autobiography.

Both Douglass and Washington were born slaves, in Maryland and Virginia. The eloquent, self-educated Douglass escaped in 1838 to become a Massachusetts day laborer, and such an effective abolitionist speaker that the Anti-Slavery Society made him its agent. Friends in England soon purchased his freedom, and in 1847 he founded his influential newspaper *North Star*. During the Civil War, Douglass helped organize a black regiment, the 54th Massachusetts, in which his two sons served. In 1899 the 72-year-old Douglass became U.S. Ambassador to Haiti.

Booker T. Washington began as a laborer in 1869 and worked his way up through the African-American educational system to become, at 25, the first principal of Tuskegee Institute. Washington was one of the ablest public speakers of his time, but his controversial argument that African-Americans should seek economic equality before social equality eventually carried him outside the mainstream civil rights movement.

#873

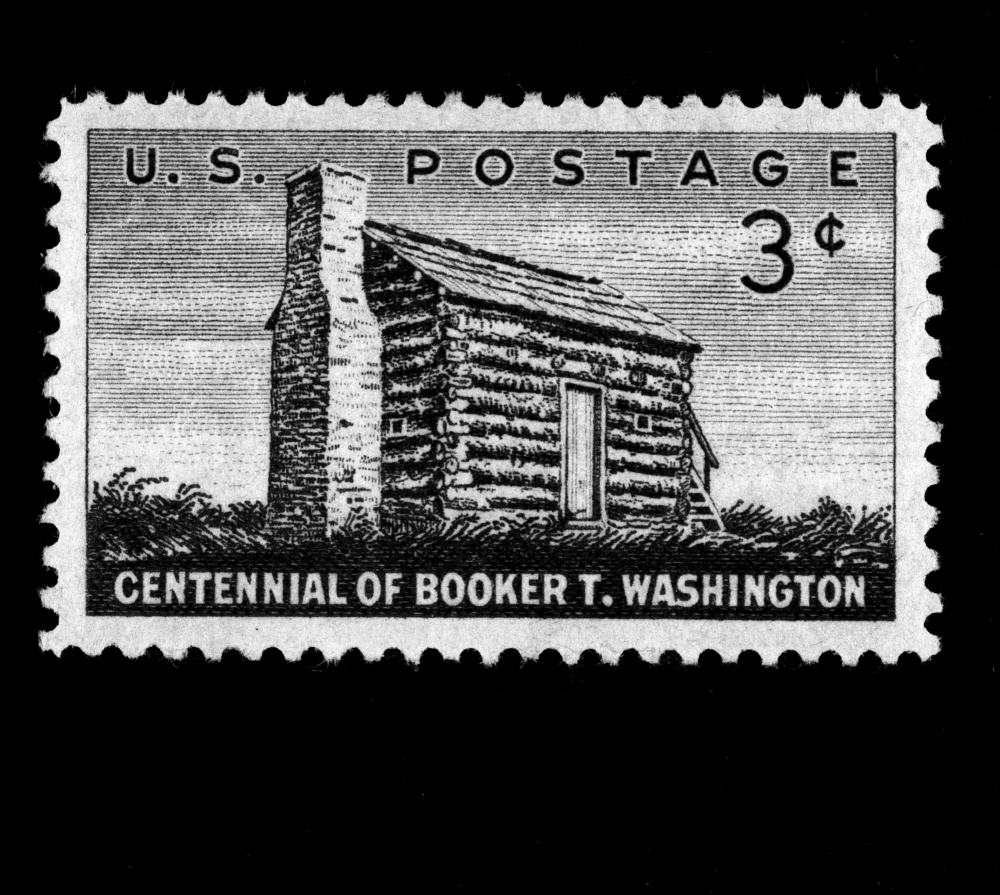

CSA #11

On October 17, 1859, President Buchanan ordered Lieutenant Colonel Robert E. Lee (#788) of the Second U.S. Cavalry to Harper's Ferry to suppress John Brown's insurrection. Lee was a career officer who had fought in Mexico and served as Superintendent of the United States Military Academy.

Eighteen months after Harper's Ferry, Lee agonized over an offer from the new president, Abraham Lincoln, to take command of all Union forces in the field. "I can anticipate no greater calamity for the country," the 54-year-old Lee responded to Lincoln, "than the dissolution of the Union. Still, a union that can only be maintained by swords and bayonets, and in which strife and civil war are to take the place of brotherly love and kindness, has no claims for me.

"If the Union is dissolved," promised Lee, "I shall return to my native State and share the miseries of my people and, save in defence, will draw my sword no more." The bombardment of Fort Sumter two months later forced Lee's hand. He forswore his oath of allegiance to the government, and left for Richmond to help Jefferson Davis (CSA #11) organize the Confederate army.

Lincoln came to regret his failure to initially arrest Lee and other career officers like J.E.B. Stuart, the skilled southern cavalry leader who was Lee's second in command at Harper's Ferry--- before they both defected. The officers were all "well known to be traitors," Lincoln explained in an 1863 letter to Erastus Corning, the mayor of Albany, N.Y., "but no one of them had then committed any crime defined in the law."

Another brilliant southern field commander was Thomas Jonathan Jackson (#788), who had left the U.S. Army in 1852. When war broke out Jackson was teaching natural philosophy at Virginia Military Institute. He was commissioned a colonel of Virginia volunteers and put in command at Harper's Ferry. A month later the 37-year-old officer was made a brigadier general.

During the first battle of Bull Run, the indomitable Jackson inspirited faltering Confederate General Bee, who thereupon called to his men, *"There is Jackson, standing like a stone wall."* The sobriquet stuck. After the battle of Chancellorsville, the last in "Stonewall" Jackson's long line of military successes, he was accidentally shot and killed by his own men. Lee lost a "good right arm."

#788

Was the United States a *union*...or a *confederation?*

To permanently resolve that divisive question, 498,332 Americans died---more than *300 a day* during the 1,500 days between the bombardment of Fort Sumter on April 12, 1861, and the last action of the Civil War on May 26, 1865.

"THE BALL IS OPENED! WAR IS INAUGURATED!" trumpeted the *New York World* on April 13 as secessionist cannon battered the Union garrison in Charleston harbor. Such headlines, both north and south, seemed almost frivolous. After so many years of violent political argument, most Americans were strangely unprepared for the agony that lay ahead.

In the North, the immediate call was for able military leaders; most of the country's experienced officers had disappeared into the Confederate Army. Only after much bloody trial and error did a handful of competent generals finally emerge who proved capable of leading brave Federal troops to victory over equally brave---and vastly outnumbered---Confederates.

Thirty-nine-year-old Ulysses Simpson Grant (#255, 787), a West Point graduate and Mexican War veteran, applied for a colonelcy in the 21st Illinois Volunteers. Seven years earlier he had been cashiered from the army for drunkenness, and supported his family by selling firewood on the streets of St. Louis and clerking in a leather store.

Like the far older Lee, Grant was a born military leader. After three years of impressive successes in the border states, Lincoln summoned Grant east and put him in command of the entire Union army. In March 1864 Congress made Grant a lieutenant general---the first U.S. officer to hold that rank since George Washington.

A few of Grant's detractors are said to have cautioned the President about the general's continued fondness for the bottle. Lincoln's reply: *"Find out what he drinks. I'd like to send a barrel of it to my other generals."* Two of Grant's abler subordinates who needed little alcoholic stimulus were 44-year-old William Tecumseh Sherman (#787), who took over Grant's former command in the west, and 34-year-old Philip Henry Sheridan (#787), who wrested control of the Shenandoah Valley from Confederate General Jubal A. Early.

After 14 months of Grant's leadership, the war was over.

#255

#787

125

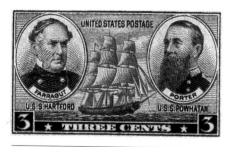

#792

Keystone of northern military strategy was economic strangulation of the South through control of the Mississippi River, plus a rigorous blockade of all major Atlantic and Gulf Coast ports.

In June 1861 southerners raised the 3,500-ton steam frigate *Merrimack*, scuttled by the North in the Norfolk Navy Yard, and rebuilt it as a metal-sheathed ram. On March 8, 1862, the renamed "*Virginia*" steamed forth against the northern fleet blockading the Chesapeake entrance. In less than three hours it rammed and sank the 30-gun *Cumberland*, set the 60-gun *Congress* afire, and scattered the rest of the Union ships.

Only the fortuitous arrival that same evening of naval genius John Ericsson's *(#628) Monitor*---a "cheese-box on a raft" from the Brooklyn Navy Yard---saved the northern blockade. The next morning, the two 11-inch guns on Ericsson's highly maneuverable *Monitor* fought the clumsy 10-gun Confederate ram to a four-hour draw. The era of the armored warship had arrived.

U.S. Navy Captain David Glasgow Farragut *(#792)* was born in Stony Point, Tennessee. When war broke out, he quit the Norfolk Navy Yard and moved north to the Hudson River Valley. The Navy Department distrusted his loyalty, and for many months withheld any assignment. In 1862 the Navy finally gave the 60-year-old Farragut command of the 17-ship West Gulf Blockading Squadron, with orders to sail 40 miles up the Mississippi and seize New Orleans.

Heavy bombardment by Farragut's floating mortars failed to reduce Forts Jackson and St. Philip below the city. On April 24 Farragut decided to run his wooden ships directly past the forts at night. The dangerous maneuver succeeded, and four days later New Orleans surrendered. Farragut's heroism two years later in the Mobile Bay minefield---"*Damn the torpedoes...go ahead...full speed!*"---is legendary. He was soon made our first admiral.

David Dixon Porter *(#792)*, son of an 1812 naval hero, was Farragut's foster brother, and commanded his mortar flotilla in the initial assault on the New Orleans forts. The 48-year-old Porter later contributed to Grant's victory at Vicksburg, and then led the North Atlantic Blockading Squadron.

After the war, as superintendent at Annapolis, Porter introduced athletics to the Naval Academy.

U.S. POSTAGE

1803   1889

JOHN ERICSSON
MEMORIAL

5 CENTS 5

"If I could save the union without freeing any slave, I would do it; if I could save it by freeing all the slaves, I would do it; and if I could do it by freeing some and leaving others alone, I would also do that."

In August 1862 Abraham Lincoln (#555) wrote those words to the influential northern journalist Horace Greeley. But the president was still playing border-state politics, respecting the property rights of slaveholders who remained loyal to the Union.

Within his cabinet Lincoln privately acknowledged the political necessity of African-American emancipation. But the government needed a clear-cut military victory, a position of strength from which it could strike a major blow at the age-old forced labor system that was helping keep the faltering Confederate economy afloat.

On September 17, 1862, at Sharpsburg, Maryland, after some of the bloodiest fighting of the Civil War, the Army of the Potomac finally gave the president the victory he needed. Union troops battered Lee's invading army down the hill, across Antietam Creek, and back into Virginia.

Five days later Abraham Lincoln issued his Preliminary Emancipation Proclamation, announcing that on the following January 1, slaves in any area still in rebellion against the United States government would thenceforth become free men and women.

As British Foreign Secretary John Earl Russell properly pointed out, the actual effect of the Emancipation Proclamation was *nil*; it freed slaves "only in those places the United States authorities cannot reach." Full legal freedom had to wait until the military defeat of the Confederacy---and the Thirteenth Amendment to a constitution that was once again the law of *all* the land (# 902).

But Abraham Lincoln's Emancipation Proclamation on New Year's Day 1863 marked a grand turning point in the quarter-millennium of African-American slavery in the United States. The president finally came to grips with the burning issue of the war: the divisive system over which the Founding Fathers and most Americans born in the century after the Revolution had agonized endlessly.

The President's proclamation marked the beginning of the end for the South's "peculiar institution."

#967

By the middle of the 19th century, contemporary warfare had become so brutal, bloody, and impersonal that even militarist governments welcomed new proposals for improved battlefield succor. In Europe, the horrible sufferings of French and Austrian wounded during the struggle for the unification of Italy inspired a Swiss philanthropist, Jean Henri Dunant, to suggest a better way to minister to the military sick and wounded, friend *and* enemy, on the battlefields of the world.

A Swiss national welfare agency picked up Dunant's idea. In 1864 it convened a meeting of representatives from 12 nations to help spread a veneer of civilization over the world's most uncivilized activity. They adopted the *Geneva Convention for the Amelioration of the Condition of the Wounded and Sick of Armies in the Field*. This new international agreement established the neutrality of medical servicemen and their civilian assistants; endorsed more humane treatment of military wounded and prisoners; and provided a new emblem to mark hospitals, medical personnel, and supplies: to honor Dunant, the colors of the Swiss flag were reversed---to create the Red Cross.

During the American Civil War, a dynamic 40-year-old ex-schoolteacher from Massachusetts, Clara Barton, also became appalled at the mounting battlefield carnage. Barton gave up her job as a clerk in the U.S. Patent Office; with government endorsement, she established a new military welfare service to supply and nurse the sick and wounded on both sides of the conflict (*#967*).

Like Florence Nightingale before her, Barton soon earned a sobriquet---*"the angel of the battlefield."* In 1865 President Lincoln authorized her to search for missing Union prisoners; she was able to identify 12,000 bodies in unmarked graves at Georgia's Andersonville prison.

During the Franco-Prussian War in 1870, Barton worked for the International Red Cross in Europe. On her return she founded the American Red Cross. As its head for the next two decades, she established the principle of Red Cross assistance in every kind of natural calamity---not just war.

Barton's proudest moment came in 1882, when, in response to years of gentle pressure, President Chester A. Arthur added the United States's name to the Geneva Convention (*#702*).

#367

On the afternoon of Good Friday, April 14th, the fifth day of peace and the last day of his life, Abraham Lincoln (#367) sat down at his desk on the ground floor of the Executive Mansion.

Certain papers required his signature: a letter concerning W. T. Howell, the Indian Agent for Michigan; a proposed list of new government employees from Maryland's Senator Cresswell and Governor Swann; nominations for a new marshal and supreme court justice for the two-year-old Idaho Territory; a plea by Thomas Geary's mother that her seventeen-year-old boy be released from the Union Army; and a petition from Confederate prisoner Benjamin F. Twilley, requesting his freedom.

As the President disposed of that small stack of correspondence, a group of sightseers gathered outside his White House window. Lincoln asked that they be sent away; then, relenting, came over and spoke to them briefly. New Hampshire Congressman Edward H. Rollins appeared in the hall with a petition for the Secretary of War. The President rested the paper on his knee, countersigned "A. *Lincoln*," and went upstairs.

Four years of guiding a terrible war had turned the former frontier wrestler and rail-splitter into into an underweight, feeble old man. He was only 56, but the unrelieved burden of sending so many young men to their death had burned him out. At times it seemed that only the unusual strength of his pen held things together. Not even the electrifying news of Lee's surrender at Appomattox could erase his haggard, haunted look.

He had led the United States through the most terrible struggle ever fought on the American continent---a dark, bloody, fratricidal conflict. For the half million who died, another quarter million returned home maimed or crippled. Reconstructing the damaged union of 36 states would be a tremendous responsibility. Many voices in the North were already crying for total vindictiveness---striking down all who had challenged the authority of the central government. More than once, the rebellion had almost brought the Union to its knees. How should its various ringleaders be punished?

In brief remarks at his second inauguration a month earlier, the President reminded everyone that the war had been fought to abolish slavery, an abomination in the eyes of the Lord---not to abolish Southerners. "*It may seem strange,*" he counseled, "that any men should dare to ask a just God's assistance in wringing their bread from the sweat of other men's faces; but let us judge not, that we be not judged." Instead of crying for vengeance, the President called for reconciliation and forgiveness---for achieving "a just and lasting peace...with malice toward none, charity for all." His audience seemed responsive.

Now he sat rocking slowly back and forth in the April twilight, brooding over all the problems that lay ahead.

Then he brightened---and thought of more pleasant hours to come. An evening at the theatre always relaxed Mary. Tonight at John T. Ford's "magnificent new Thespian temple" a few blocks away from the White House on Tenth Street, comedienne Laura Keane would play "Florence Trenchard" in Our American Cousin, a broad farce ridiculing British manners. The President and Mary had seen the popular Tom Taylor play several times before, but characters like the boisterous "Asa Trenchard" and stuffy "Lord Dundreary" could always coax forth a smile.

General Grant had come up to Washington to issue peacetime orders for the army. He and his wife had been invited to join the theatre party. But the day before, in a typically unpredictable show of temperament, Mary had inexcusably and publicly humiliated Julia Grant. Now the Grants took the opportunity to plead a desire to visit their neglected children at school in New Jersey.

When the President heard that Ulysses was not coming, he almost withdrew. But in the Grants' place, Mary had invited Clara Harris, daughter of New York Senator Ira Harris, and her fiancé, Major Henry R. Rathbone. It was too late for even the President to change everyone's plans.

It grew dark, and an aide wandered into Lincoln's study, reporting that Ford was feverishly redecorating the theatre for his honored visitors. The upholstered Presidential rocker was already in place in the double box. After dinner, as the group prepared to leave the White House, the President encountered one last persistent office-seeker, George Ashmun, in the doorway. He scribbled a note for the policeman-doorkeeper: "Allow Mr. Ashmun & friend to come in at 9. A.M. to-morrow."

Then Abraham Lincoln put on his tall black hat and stepped out into the gusty April evening (#571).

#571

#784

African-American men gained the right to vote in 1870; African-American (and white) *women* had to wait another 50 years. Not until the 20th century did the woman's rights movement in the United States develop from the early efforts of a few brave females, into several state-led campaigns for suffrage.

Lucretia Coffin Mott (#959) came from an old Nantucket Quaker family. In the early 1800s, she, as well as fellow-activist Susan Brownell Anthony (#784), gave up teaching careers to concern themselves with such social causes as temperance, abolition, labor rights---and votes for women. In areas of reform invariably dominated by men, they were forced to organize counterpart groups, like Mott's Philadelphia Female Anti-Slavery Society, and Anthony's Daughters of Temperance.

In 1840 Mott, with her brilliant orator and journalist friend Elizabeth Cady Stanton (#959), attended an anti-slavery convention in London. While their husbands were welcome to the floor, the women were barred. Their indignation merely caused them to redouble domestic efforts to establish a national woman's rights movement. A milestone was the July 1848 convention in Seneca Falls, N.Y., where Stanton introduced a bill of rights for women.

In the years after the Civil War, Stanton helped organize the National Woman Suffrage Association, which fought for legal, political, and industrial equality (and also for liberal divorce laws). She led the group for two decades, and together with Anthony edited its militant feminist weekly newspaper *The Revolution*. Its motto was, "Men, *their rights and nothing more. Women, their rights and nothing less.*"

In the presidential election of 1872, the 52-year-old Anthony, citing the 14th Amendment, led a group of Rochester women attempting to vote for Horace Greeley. She was arrested and fined $100, which was never paid.

Carrie Chapman Lane Catt (#959) was a midwesterner who worked tirelessly for woman's suffrage. At 41 she took over leadership of the National American Woman Suffrage Association, and continued its long struggle through ratification ---in 1920---of the 19th Amendment, finally giving women the vote. Catt subsequently lent her great influence to the fight for woman's rights around the world.

THE

HOMEST

ACT

1862

#1134

Petroleum had been seeping out of ancient Devonian rocks in northwestern Pennsylvania for almost 400 million years. Native Americans used the greasy oil for magic rites, body paints, and medicine. Imitative settlers were soon dosing themselves with health tonics the pitchmen called *Seneca Oil* or *Genessee Oil*.

To make the black ooze more easily accessible, an ex-railroad conductor named Edwin Laurentine Drake drilled what he hoped would be an artesian oil well, at Oil Creek near Titusville, Pennsylvania, 40 miles south of Lake Erie. On August 27, 1859, only 69 feet down, Drake brought in the first U.S. "gusher" (*#1134*). Four years later in Cleveland, John D. Rockefeller entered the oil business with his first refinery.

Refined petroleum, mainly in the form of millions of barrels of inexpensive kerosene, quickly provided America with its newest home lighting fuel. The whale oil fishery was destroyed.

Further developments in refining paved the way for the internal combustion engine. American automobiles, tractors, trucks, locomotives, and airplanes would eventually be designed around combustion of distilled petroleum products. In addition to fuel and lubricants, the world soon discovered that petroleum's complex hydrocarbon molecules could also be rearranged to create dyes, drugs, and indispensable plastics.

Following early attempts to use steam and even electricity (*#296a*) for motive power, the first operational road vehicle using an internal combustion engine was a three-wheeled German car built in 1885 by Karl Benz. By 1894 Daimler's French Panhard displayed the basic features of today's automobile. The following year the American inventor George Selden received a United States patent on his two-cycle automobile engine; it dominated the rapidly expanding American car market for a quarter century.

Not until 1911 did Henry Ford (*#1286A*) break Selden's patent by convincing the United States Supreme Court that his own Model T *four*-cycle engine was a completely different invention. By then Detroit was on its way to becoming the undisputed center of the world automotive industry; Ford's "Tin Lizzies" were rolling off primitive assembly lines fast enough to make him the pre-eminent automobile manufacturer. In 1913 Ford sold a quarter of a million cars.

The American road lay wide open before him.

#1286A

#296a

#Q5- Q

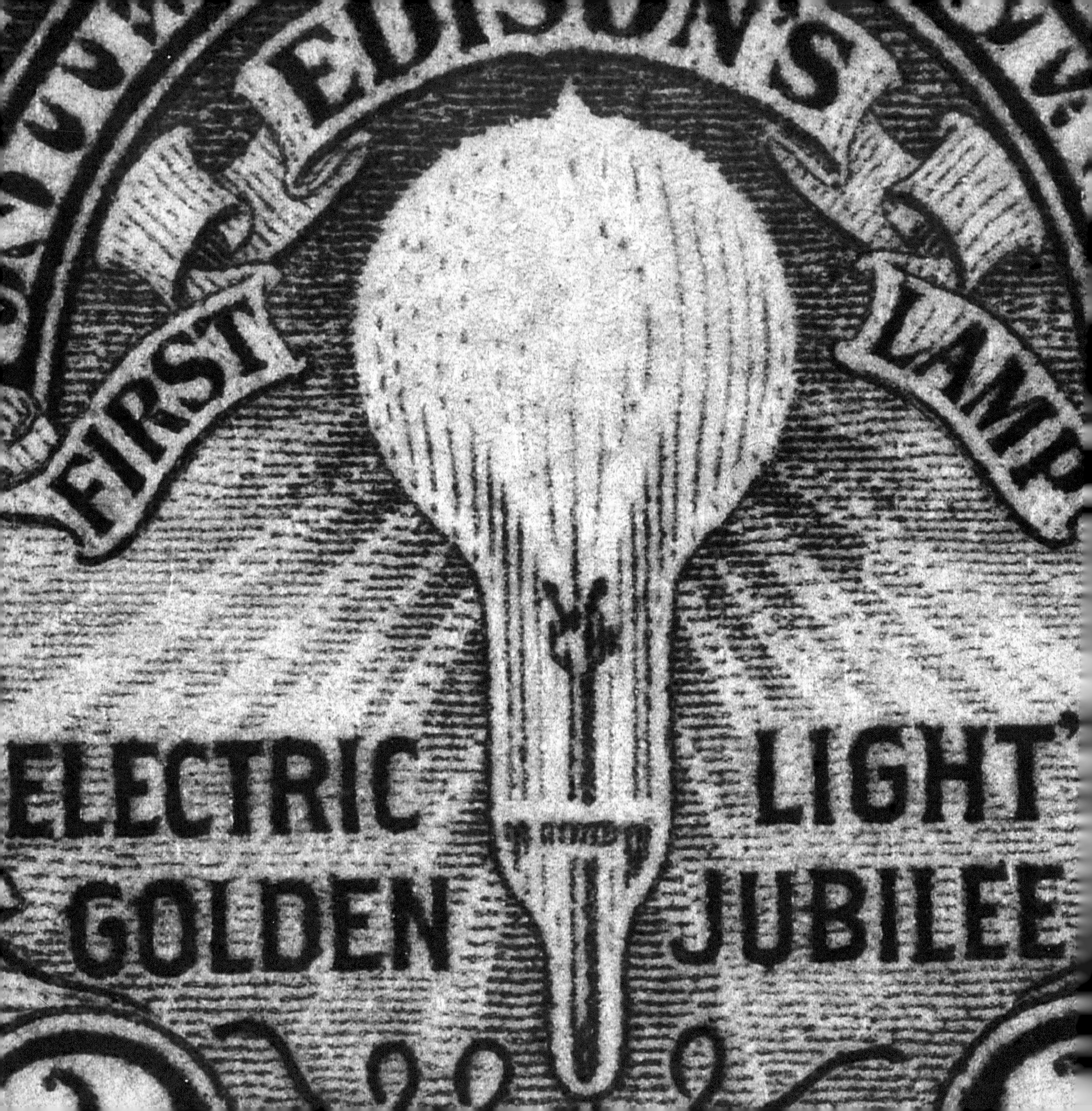

EDISON'S

FIRST

LAMP

FIRST

ELECTRIC   LIGHT

GOLDEN   JUBILEE

THE CREATIVE SPIRITS

For a fertile and inquiring mind tempered by common sense, no one could beat Ben Franklin (#803, 1073).

When he wasn't printing newspapers, writing almanacs, selling books, or founding libraries, schools, and learned societies, Franklin was a tireless tinkerer. Unlike other 18th century savants who were more interested in logic than experimentation, Franklin possessed an unparalleled curiosity and enthusiasm for the practical aspects of scientific research.

He looked at America's fireplaces, and decided they heated the chimney instead of the room, so he invented an efficient cast-iron stove, plus a smokeless chimney.

As a deputy Postmaster General for the colonies, he completely reorganized that service. He also studied postal reports of destructive storms at Charleston, Philadelphia, New York, and Boston---and decided they were the *same* storm, moving up the coast. He had discovered the hurricane track.

Before anyone considered the logic and value of municipal services, Franklin introduced hospitals, fire protection, and paved, clean, well-lit streets to Philadelphia.

He compiled ocean temperature records and "discovered" the warm Gulf Stream, sweeping northeast along the Atlantic Coast from the Bahamas to the Grand Banks. Sailing captains welcomed Franklin's new charts. Navigating by ocean temperatures, they were able to shave days off their voyages.

Early theories to explain the phenomenon called "*electricity*" were unsatisfactory, so Franklin experimented with a new Dutch condensing jar. He sent up a kite into a lightning storm, and announced that lightning and electricity were the same thing. Others may have thought they were identical---Franklin proved it (and was lucky he didn't get electrocuted).

Then he attached a metal rod to the tops of homes, farmhouses, and barns. The rod led lightning harmlessly down into the ground. It made *"Franklin"* a household name throughout the world; Louis XV of France sent him a personal note of thanks.

"Poor Richard" also had valid ideas about the origin of earthquakes, the *aurora borealis*, and the common cold.

At 42, Franklin retired from business. Before long he was America's greatest statesman-diplomat. When old age interfered with his reading, he invented bifocals.

#372

Robert Fulton, born near Lancaster, Pennsylvania, ten years before the American Revolution, was a portrait painter and an able mechanic with a penchant for perfecting other inventors' most promising ideas. In 1801 he tried unsuccessfully to sell the French and British his own version of the submarine-and-torpedo concept pioneered by David Bushnell 25 years earlier. Fulton also perfected canal improvements, and machines for spinning flax, making ropes, and sawing and polishing marble.

He entered the American pantheon as the mythical "inventor of the steamboat" in 1807 when his influential partner Robert R. Livingston contracted Fulton to build a paddlewheeler to service the 20-year Hudson River steamboat monopoly Livingston had wangled from the New York State legislature.

Fulton brought up the rear of a long line of steamboat developers, including Rumsey, Fitch, Morey, Read, Stevens, and Symington (whose practical success Fulton had personally witnessed in England). Before long his 150-foot-long, 13-foot-wide successful commercial steamboat *Clermont* (#372), powered by a custom-built British steam engine, was splashing the 150 miles from New York City to Albany in 32 hours. His patron Livingston spent most of his time in federal court, unsuccessfully attempting to project his Hudson River monopoly onto every navigable river in the United States.

Robert McCormick, a Shenandoah Valley blacksmith, was a prolific inventor of labor-saving farm machinery. For 20 years he tried unsuccessfully to perfect a grain harvester. Picking up that challenge in the late 1820s, his son Cyrus Hall McCormick (#891) soon designed a sophisticated horse-drawn reaper that combined a platform, guards, main drive wheel, serrated reciprocating knife, revolving reel, and grain divider. It was used successfully for the first time in the harvest of 1831.

Battling competition while continuing to improve his reaper, McCormick eventually opened a huge Chicago factory to satisfy the exploding agricultural needs of the Midwest. An astute and aggressive businessman, he bought and added to his design a patented self-rake, twine binder, and other improvements. McCormick soon accumulated an enormous personal fortune, selling his reaper all over the world.

#891

#889

Eli Whitney (#889) was born in Massachusetts a decade before the Revolution. Visiting Georgia in 1793, he began doodling with a simple device to extract seeds from short-staple cotton fibers. In only ten days Whitney had invented his "*cotton engine*"; it led to a vast expansion of southern cotton-growing. His patented design was pirated, and Whitney suffered through years of litigation. In 1798 he established a profitable Connecticut firearms factory, the first American workplace to utilize the division of labor, with standardized, interchangeable parts.

❧

Elias Howe (#892) was another Yankee tinkerer, also born in Massachusetts. In 1838, while working in a Boston machine shop, Howe perfected a hand-cranked mechanical device to sew leather and cloth. No one in the United States seemed interested, so Howe carried his "*sewing machine*" to England, where he turned it into a major marketing success. When Howe finally returned home, he was dismayed to find an army of patent infringers. His years of litigation were finally successful.

#892

❧

#945

Thomas Alva Edison (#945) was the quintessential American inventor-businessman, determined to exploit the full market potential of every one of his scientific inspirations. Born in Ohio in 1845, Edison received only three months schooling, but clambered up from newsboy and telegraph operator to the proprietorship, at age 29, of a New Jersey experimental workshop. It was the forerunner of the modern research laboratory, in which teams of workers systematically investigate applied science.

Edison's development of early phonograph recording, incandescent lighting (#654), electric power distribution, and motion and talking pictures, were merely the highlights of a well-publicized inventive career that spanned more than half a century. At his death in 1931, Edison held 1,033 patents.

❧

George Eastman (#1062) was born in upstate New York two decades before the Civil War. He was 26 years old when he invented a process to replace cumbersome wet-plate photography. Ten years later he devised a standardized film roll and simple camera. Eastman's "Kodak"---"*You Press the Button, We Do the Rest!*"---changed the way the world looks (and smiles) at itself.

#1062

#875

Crawford Williamson Long (#875) received his medical degree from the University of Pennsylvania in 1839, and worked for a year and a half in New York City hospitals. Establishing a practice in Georgia, Dr. Long began experimenting with surgical anesthetics. In 1842, the 27-year-old doctor employed ethyl ether to supress pain during an operation to remove a neck tumor.

Long failed to publicize his successful procedure, and credit for initial surgical use of ether was temporarily assigned to a Boston dentist, William Thomas Green Morton: in 1846, also at the age of 27, Dr. Morton administered ethyl ether during an operation at Massachusetts General Hospital.

Luther Burbank (#876), born in Massachusetts in 1849, was an agricultural scientist who made the world a little prettier and helped it eat better. A century before gene-splicing, Burbank was America's most famous plant breeder. At the age of 26 he established an agricultural research station in California. Over the next 50 years, he developed countless new varieties of apples, peaches, plums, nectarines, quinces, raspberries, and blackberries.

Burbank's experiments with edible plants created vastly improved strains of potatoes, tomatoes, corn, peas, squash, and asparagus. He developed a spineless cactus for feeding cattle--- plus new varieties of lilies, and the well-known Shasta daisy.

George Washington Carver (#953) was an illustrious agricultural chemist, born of African-American slave parents in Missouri around the end of the Civil War---the exact date is unknown. Carver worked his way through Iowa State College, and in 1894 joined the teaching staff at Tuskegee Institute. Two years later he was made Tuskegee's director of agricultural research, a post he held for the rest of his life.

Carver gained international fame with brilliant contributions to southern soil improvement through crop rotation and diversification, and for developing hundreds of new industrial uses for such southern agricultural staples as peanuts, soybeans, and sweet potatoes. He devised valuable by-product usage for cotton waste, and also demonstrated methods of extracting important industrial pigments from southern clays.

He showed us how to turn humble elements into gold.

#876

#864

Henry Wadsworth Longfellow (#864) was born in Maine in 1807. He was well-educated, and taught for several years at Bowdoin College; at 29 he became a modern language professor at Harvard. Following the death of his first wife, Longfellow traveled extensively in Europe, remarried, wrote such well-known poems as *The Village Blacksmith, Excelsior, The Wreck of the Hesperus,* and *The Children's Hour.* At 40 he began work on a series of immensely popular long narrative poems that soon established him as America's unofficial "poet laureate": *Evangeline, The Song of Hiawatha, The Courtship of Miles Standish,* and *Paul Revere's Ride.*

Although Longfellow earned substantial academic respect, mass acclaim, and some wealth during the rest of his life, his lyric style is a bit sentimental when measured against today's tastes:

> And a verse of a Lapland song
> Is haunting my memory still:
> "A boy's will is the wind's will,
> And the thoughts of youth are long, long thoughts."

John Greenleaf Whittier (#865) was born the same year as Longfellow; he outlived him by 10 years. A farmer's son from Massachusetts, Whittier had little formal education, but was an omnivorous reader. In his early teens, he was inspired by the poetry of Burns, and began to contribute his own work to local newspapers; at 31 he was able to publish a book of poetry. In conventional meter and rhyme, Whittier's poems accurately reflect aspects of rural life in New England before mill-town industrialization.

Mainly remembered as a genial and gentle poet, in his early years Whittier was a fiery abolitionist editor, a fighter for temperance, peace, and woman's suffrage. After the Civil War, he wrote almost a hundred hymns, including *Dear Lord and Father of Mankind.* Whittier's most famous poems are such joyous celebrations of the New England countryside as *Snow-bound, Maud Muller,* and the immortal *Barefoot Boy:*

> Oh for boyhood's painless play,
> Sleep that wakes in laughing day,
> Health that mocks the doctor's rules,
> Knowledge never learned in schools.

#865

James Russell Lowell (#866) was born in Cambridge in 1819, and died a year before Whittier. He graduated Harvard Law School at 21. Abandoning the law for literature, he helped found a magazine that failed after a few issues. Lowell mixed his sentimental poetry with stinging satire, establishing his reputation through a series of lampoons, *The Biglow Papers*.

Lowell was a fervent abolitionist and a vehement opponent of the Mexican War. He mixed poetry with political diatribes; the public loved it. At 36 he succeeded Longfellow as head of Harvard's modern language department, and two years later became the first editor of the *Atlantic Monthly*. A dozen years after the Civil War, Lowell was named U.S. Minister to Spain; three years later he was transferred to the same post in London. Lowell's incisive and amusing critical writing did much to increase foreign respect for American letters.

> *And what is so rare as a day in June?*
> *Then, if ever, come perfect days;*
> *Then Heaven tries earth if it be in tune.*
> *And over it softly her warm ear lays…*

Walt Whitman (#867) was born on Long Island the same year as Lowell, and died the same year as Whittier.

Much of Whitman's work heralds democracy and extols the dignity of the common man. He was a struggling 28-year-old newspaperman when he began to write 12 unusual poems, self-published eight years later as *Leaves of Grass*. Their innovative form and content brought him immediate attention, not all of it favorable---plus an unexpected and influential letter of praise from Emerson, who called the book, "*The most extraordinary piece of wit and wisdom America has yet contributed.*" That generous encouragement from the Sage of Concord proved prophetic; today Whitman is generally considered America's greatest poet.

During the Civil War, Whitman worked in Washington as a volunteer hospital nurse, while continuing to write poetry. His poems include two on the death of Lincoln, *O Captain! My Captain!* and *When Lilacs Last in the Dooryard Bloom'd*:

> *When lilacs last in the dooryard bloom'd*
> *And the great star early droop'd in the western sky in the night,*
> *I mourn'd, and yet shall mourn with ever-returning spring.*

#866

#867

#874

America's great artist-ornithologist, John James Audubon (#874), was born in Haiti in 1785, the son of a wealthy French naval officer and planter. Because his mother was unwed and a Creole, Audubon always fudged the place and date of his birth.

Raised in France by an adoring stepmother, Audubon came to the United States on family business when he was 18 years old. From childhood he had always been a bird lover, carefully observing and recording bird behavior, and performing early banding experiments.

At 23 Audubon married and moved to Kentucky, and later to Louisiana, where his devoted wife Lucy eked out a living teaching school, while Audubon painted portraits. His fascination with birds continued. In 1826, he sailed to England to find patrons and subscribers for a unique and splendid project, several hundred huge hand-colored engravings to be called *The Birds of America*, with a five-volume *Ornithological Biography*.

Audubon's genius was immediately recognized, and he returned home with sufficient funds to begin 11 years of work on his monumental undertaking, including expeditions to collect specimens for the precise and lovely drawings later engraved onto copper by Robert Havell, Jr.

While a few of Audubon's more flamboyant executions may trouble the most fastidious ornithologist or artist, his rare amalgam of scientific observation and graphic skill gave America one of its best-loved intellectual achievements.

❧

Audubon's dramatic North American "*Columbia Jay*," reproduced on this 5¢ stamp in 1963 (*#1241*), is actually a Collie's magpie-jay and only native to western Mexico. The magnificent black-throated bird, a gift to Audubon, was reportedly collected along the Columbia River in the Pacific Northwest. In this instance, Audubon wavered from his resolution never to draw a bird he had not personally collected. As a result the Mexican jay is out of place among the 435 copperplate engravings in Audubon's masterpiece "elephant folio" collection.

The Post Office knew all along that the bird was a Mexican jay, but the color and perfect rectangular proportions seemed too good to pass up. It still calls *#1241* "one of the most highly regarded stamps ever issued."

#859

Washington Irving (#859), widely considered America's earliest man of letters, was born in New York City during the last year of the Revolution. He grew up in a busy literary atmosphere. At 26, under the pen name *"Diedrich Knickerbocker,"* Irving wrote a witty *History of New York from the Beginning of the World to the End of the Dutch Dynasty.* It was America's first important whimsical literary work.

When the Irving family hardware business failed, the young author devoted all his professional time to writing. In *The Sketch Book of Geoffrey Crayon, Gent.*, Irving won immediate fame with such immortal Hudson Valley tales as *Rip van Winkle* and *The Legend of Sleepy Hollow.*

Invited to the American embassy in Madrid in 1826 to write a history of Columbus, based on papers collected by Martin Fernández de Navarré, Irving also busied himself on other Spanish themes.

After extensive European travel, Irving returned to his beloved Hudson River estate *Sunnyside.* But soon he was again posted to Madrid, this time as U.S. Minister. Irving completed his lengthy biography of George Washington at *Sunnyside,* shortly before his death in 1859.

James Fenimore Cooper (#860) was born in New Jersey six years after the Revolution. He was a young retired naval officer of 31 when he began his writing career. Legend relates how Cooper tossed an English novel into the fire, assuring his wealthy wife he could produce better work. His first attempt was a dismal failure, but a year later *The Spy*, a long and tangled tale of New York State Revolutionary guerrilla warfare, gained instant popularity at home and abroad; it was even translated into Russian.

Whereupon Cooper began to assiduously mine the colonial history of the northeastern frontier with novel after novel containing extravagant, highly romanticized portraits of English pioneers and their friends and enemies.

A half century later, Mark Twain, whose experience with native Americans was somewhat broader than that of the author of *Leatherstocking Tales*, gibed that *"the difference between a Cooper Indian, and the Indian that stands in front of the cigar-store, is not spacious."*

#860

The real life of Edgar Allan Poe (#986) has always set a poor example for America's youth. But what a writer!

Poe was born in Boston in 1809. His parents were impecunious actors who died while he was a baby. Poe was adopted by his wealthy southern godfather, John Allan. During Poe's freshman year at the University of Virginia, he incurred large gambling debts; Allan disinherited him, and the young man was forced to leave school. At 21, Poe was accepted at West Point. Within three months he was expelled for "gross neglect of duty." To keep from starving, Poe began to write.

For the rest of his life, Poe was an alcoholic and drug addict, beset by fits of depression and melancholia. He moved to Baltimore, tried to poison himself; then married his 13-year-old cousin---who died at 24.

Despite very real personal problems, Poe possessed a clear and analytic mind. He was a superb editor, incisive literary critic, a poet of narrow but passionate skills, and a first-rate author whose dream-like, often macabre stories outdid the English romanticists. He died in Baltimore in 1849 during an alcoholic binge, leaving behind an original body of work that marks him as one of America's authentic geniuses.

❧

Louisa May Alcott (#862), born in 1832, was one of four sisters in a distinguished but impoverished Concord, Massachusetts, family. As a young girl Alcott knew and conversed with Emerson and Thoreau. Her first book *Flower Fables*, published when she was 22, was created from sketches originally written as babysitting diversions for Emerson's daughter Ellen.

"The sharp disciplines of poverty and pain made me strong," Alcott later wrote. To her delight, her poems and stories were soon appearing in the *Atlantic Monthly* and other periodicals, adding a welcome supplement to the family income.

An ardent fighter for abolition and woman's suffrage, Alcott also served as a nurse during the Civil War. Her 1863 book *Hospital Sketches*, based on wartime experiences (which undermined her health), was warmly received. In 1868 she published the perceptive and largely autobiographical classic *Little Women*, soon followed by her equally successful *Little Men* and *Jo's Boys*. All remain perennial children's favorites.

THOREAU

U.S. 5 cents

#1327

Ralph Waldo Emerson (#861) was born in Boston in 1803. At his death 79 years later, he was revered as one of America's most original and profound thinkers.

Emerson came from a bookish family. His erudite father, minister of Boston's First Unitarian Church, died when Emerson was eight. The intellectual care of the boy was turned over to a brilliant aunt, who helped shape Emerson's independent mind.

Graduating from Harvard Divinity School, Emerson became pastor of Boston's Old North Church in 1829. He married, but his wife soon died. Emerson's distress and inner conflict led him to resign his pastorate in 1832, and he traveled extensively abroad, meeting Carlyle, Coleridge, and Wordsworth. Such literary contacts, plus his reading in eastern and mystic philosophy, stirred the development of his unique transcendental outlook---based on natural reason rather than experience.

When Emerson returned home in 1835 to settle among friends at Concord, he remarried, and began an active new career as scholar, writer, poet, and lecturer. His remaining half century was filled with intense intellectual activity: far-ranging lecture tours; provocative, often highly controversial speeches; editorships; political arguments (Emerson was an active abolitionist); poetry writing; and publishing many influential critical essays.

Emerson's young neighbor, friend, confidant, and handyman-caretaker was Henry David Thoreau (#1327). Thoreau graduated from Harvard around the time Emerson settled in Concord. Thoreau, too, was an essayist and poet, on his way to becoming America's most famous naturalist.

In 1845 at the age of 28, Thoreau built a tiny cabin on the shores of Walden Pond near Concord, where he lived for two years in contemplative isolation, observing nature through the changing seasons, and "sucking out all the marrow of life." The experience was carefully recorded in *Walden; or Life in the Woods*, one of Thoreau's several classic works on nature and philosophy.

Thoreau's later *Essay on Civil Disobedience*, provoked by the Mexican War, marked him as a great champion of the eternal struggle of the independent-minded individual against repressive social organization. He died at 45.

#293

With a stroke of the pen on March 20, 1861, Abraham Lincoln ---no mean writer himself---probably changed the course of American literature. He crossed out the recommendation *"W.L. Brown, Ia."* as Secretary for the three-week-old Territory of Nevada, and substituted *"Orion Clemens---Mo."* instead. For *his own* secretary, Orion brought along younger brother Sam Clemens, who soon found a new career writing pseudonymous funny articles for the Virginia City, Nevada, *Territorial Enterprise.*

"Mark Twain" (#863)---born Samuel Langhorne Clemens in Florida, Missouri in 1835---was about as far from the New England literary tradition as you can get. He began his career as a journeyman typesetter along the Mississippi, occasionally dreaming up humorous local "fillers" for newspaper columns.

In 1857 Sam Clemens decided to make his fortune in South America. But he tarried at New Orleans, and for 18 months served as apprentice to a Mississippi River pilot (#293). Sam's later pseudonym came from the leadsman's cry *"Mark twain!"* indicating two fathoms of safe water.

When the Civil War disrupted steamboat traffic on the Mississippi, 27-year-old Clemens accompanied his brother to Nevada. Three years later, working on a San Francisco newspaper, Twain emerged as an imaginative Western humorist. His famous short story, *The Celebrated Jumping Frog of Calaveras County,* appeared in New York City's *Saturday Press* in 1865. It was universally reprinted. "Mark Twain's" future was assured.

Twain's next 43 years were filled with travel, lectures, and refreshingly unconventional writing. *The Innocents Abroad, A Tramp Abroad,* and *Following the Equator* offer amusing sketches of middle-class Americans on "grand tours." *Roughing It* and *Life on the Mississippi* are autobiographical accounts of riverboating and early days in the West. *A Connecticut Yankee in King Arthur's Court* and *Pudd'nhead Wilson* are irreverent novels.

But Twain's masterworks are his timeless books for children. As nostalgic evocations of his own boyhood, *Tom Sawyer* and the deceptively innocent *Huckleberry Finn* blend simplicity with deep social insight. As Twain---and America---grew older, the amusing professional writer became the pessimistic critic. But who will ever forget Aunt Polly's introductory cry: *"'Tom! What's gone with that boy, I wonder? You, TOM!'* No answer."

James Abbott McNeill Whistler (#885), born in Massachusetts in 1834, always insisted on "art for art's sake." His father was a U.S. military engineer who helped construct the first railway in Russia. He took Whistler to St. Petersburg, where the boy received early drawing lessons---apparently good ones.

In his late teens, Whistler was dropped from West Point for failing chemistry, and was later tossed out of the U.S. Coast and Geodetic Survey for etching doodles on his map plates. He decided to become a painter, and at 21 left for Paris, where he came under the influence of the French impressionists, including Courbet and Manet.

Whistler was soon painting in an individualistic and highly decorative style that combined abstract color harmonies with influences of recently introduced Japanese prints. He slowly gained recognition as a fine draftsman of great technical ability, turning out highly original works that foreshadowed many subsequent painting styles and movements.

Moving to London in 1869, Whistler attempted to speed up his public acceptance with elaborate publicity and lawsuits. The Pre-Raphaelite artist Dante Gabriel Rossetti wrote:

> *A touchy young painter named Whistler*
> *In every respect is a bristler:*
> *A tube of white lead*
> *Or a punch in the head*
> *Come equally handy to Whistler.*

A bitter polemicist, his most famous legal action, for libel, was brought against critic John Ruskin, who characterized Whistler's *Nocturne in Black and Gold: The Falling Rocket* as "flinging a pot of paint in the public's face."

The American painter won the suit, but the court awarded him only a farthing's damages, and denied legal costs. Whistler was bankrupt, but continued to defend the fluid, delicate style of *Nocturne in Black and Gold* as an aesthetic "arrangement of light, form, and color." His most famous "arrangement," painted in 1872---*Arrangement In Gray and Black*, or *Mrs. George Washington Whistler*, often called *Whistler's Mother* (#737)---now hangs in the Louvre. In 1934, a U.S. stamp designer trimmed the artist's composition, adding a vase of flowers at the bottom "for balance."

Whistler would have punched him in the head.

#884

Gilbert Charles Stuart (#884), was born in Rhode Island 20 years before the Revolution. He specialized in painting elegant portraits of sitters with ruddy complexions. Stuart's three canvases of George Washington, all painted from life during the President's second term, are American icons.

Stuart showed an early aptitude for drawing, and studied briefly in Edinburgh with a well-known Scots painter. He was greatly influenced by Reynolds and Gainsborough. After a lengthy visit home, he became a London protegé of the famous expatriate American painter, Benjamin West, 17 years his senior. During the early years of the Revolution, Stuart worked in West's London studio, where he painted King George III, as well as his masterpiece *Portrait of a Gentleman Skating*.

In 1792, Stuart returned to United States and settled in Boston, where he was honored as the finest and most prolific American portrait painter: he painted a host of famous sitters in multiple copies. At one-year intervals Stuart was commissioned to paint his three famous life portraits of Washington. The last, unfinished, is immortalized on the dollar bill (#707). It was ordered by the President's wife---but Martha had to settle for one of Stuart's 75 copies; the painter kept the original (now in Boston's Museum of Fine Arts) for himself.

Augustus Saint-Gaudens (#886) was born in Ireland in 1848 and was brought to New York as an infant. Apprenticed to a cameo cutter, he soon mastered the art of carving in low relief, and embarked on a career that would make him America's most famous sculptor. After studying at Cooper Union and the National Academy of Design, Saint-Gaudens was accepted at the Beaux Arts academy in Paris, and afterwards spent three years in Italy absorbing the art of the Renaissance and producing his first major sculpture, *Hiawatha*.

Saint-Gaudens's design for a statue of Admiral Farragut, unveiled in New York City when the sculptor was 33 years old, reflected his simplicity, good taste, and technical ability. It set new standards for American public art. Saint-Gaudens was honored with important municipal and private commissions, and is represented by impressive statues, monuments, and memorials in many American and European cities and parks.

#886

The sculptor Daniel Chester French (#887), son of an assistant Secretary of the Treasury, was born in New Hampshire. Two years Saint-Gaudens's junior, French studied sculpture in Boston and Italy. Only 22 years old and relatively untrained, he won the competition for a centennial statue at Concord Bridge. At its dedication in 1875, a stanza from his neighbor Emerson's "*Concord Hymn*" was carved into the pedestal of *The Minute Man*:

> *By the rude bridge that arched the flood,*
> *Their flag to April's breeze unfurled,*
> *Here once the embattled farmers stood*
> *And fired the shot heard round the world.*

French's statue has become a revered symbol of America's indomitable military response. It was featured on a 5¢ stamp (#619) for the 1925 Revolutionary sesquicentennial, and also appeared on World War II posters, war bonds, and savings stamps.

French's style, alternating detailed realism with sweeping allegory, won him a steady flow of public monument commissions in major cities throughout the United States. His better-known works include Columbia University's *Alma Mater*, a bust of Emerson, and a statue of John Harvard at Cambridge. Until the completion of Mt. Rushmore (#1011), French's 64-foot-high *The Republic*, created for the 1893 World's Columbian Exposition, held the distinction of being the tallest sculpture executed in America. French's crowning achievement is his great marble figure of the seated Lincoln in the Memorial at Washington, D.C.

Frederic Remington (#888), artist, illustrator, and sculptor, was born in upstate New York in 1861. He studied at Yale's School of Fine Arts. Much of Remington's spirited work is devoted to themes he encountered on therapeutic visits to the Western plains; cowboys, native Americans, and U.S. cavalrymen. Replicas of Remington's 23 bronze sculptures in that genre are included in most U.S. museum collections.

#888

Remington was amazingly prolific, turning out thousands of drawings, magazine illustrations, and paintings during a relatively short life---he died in his late 40s. In the Spanish-American War, Remington accompanied U.S. troops to Cuba, filing stories and sketches for the Hearst newspaper chain to add a feeling of Western glamor to that somewhat one-sided conflict.

#879

You can have kings, give me the music-makers…
---POPULAR 1940s' SONG

Stephen Collins Foster (#879) was born near Pittsburgh in 1826. His Scotch-Irish parents recognized the boy's musical talent when he was six years old, but afforded him no formal musical education. After an attempt at college, and four years' work in Cincinnati as a bookkeeper, Foster began to write "Ethiopian songs" out of his head. He was following the popular *"Zip Coon"* minstrel show genre, launched by Dan Emmett when Foster was seventeen years old.

In his own musical versions, however, Foster substituted sentiment for African-American caricature. His technical understanding of composition was slim, but he had a keen ear for a felicitous turn of phrase, plus an outstanding ability to neatly polish his original melodic sketches.

Unfortunately Foster was a spectacularly poor businessman. Even though he professionally outshone all of his songwriting colleagues, he sold for a pittance publishing rights to some of his best drawing-room ballads. After 1860 Foster was reduced to grinding out undistinguished potboilers.

But in less than a dozen years he had written such "all-time American favorites" as *Oh! Susannah, Swanee River, My Old Kentucky Home, Massa's in the Cold, Cold Ground, The Old Folks at Home, Old Dog Tray, Jeanie With the Light Brown Hair, Nelly Bly,* and just before the Civil War, yet one more romantic view of the Southland, *Old Black Joe.* Four years later, at age 38, Foster was dead of acute alcoholism in New York City's Bellevue Hospital.

John Philip Sousa (#880), whom British musical circles affectionately dubbed *"The March King,"* was born in Washington, D.C., in 1854. Like Foster, Sousa also demonstrated musical promise at the age of six, and soon began to study the violin, harmony, and composition.

During Sousa's apprenticeship with the band of the United States Marine Corps, of which his father was a member, he learned to play many other instruments. In 1880, the 26-year-old Sousa was made bandmaster of the Marine Band, a post he held for a dozen years.

#880

In 1892 Sousa left the Corps to establish his own band, which he conducted on several triumphal world concert tours. An indefatigable composer of operas, songs, and suites, Sousa also wrote almost 100 marches, including such enormously popular pieces as *The Stars and Stripes Forever, Liberty Bell, The Washington Post March,* and *Semper Fidelis.*

#881

Victor Herbert (#881) was born in Dublin, Ireland, in 1859. He studied composition in Germany, and became a virtuoso cellist. In 1886, the Metropolitan Opera invited the 27-year-old Herbert to New York to be its first cellist, with his wife as a *prima donna.* Herbert also composed cello concertos for the New York Philharmonic, serving as soloist.

After a dozen years Herbert left the Metropolitan to become conductor of the Pittsburgh Symphony Orchestra, and began to write serious operas which were not well received. Switching to operettas, Herbert found his metier. From 1903 to 1917, he composed the immensely popular *Babes in Toyland, Naughty Marietta, Sweethearts,* and *The Red Mill*---all of which eventually became grist for Hollywood's own motion picture musical mill.

Herbert was a leader in the fight for musical copyright legislation, and helped found ASCAP---the American Society of Composers, Authors, and Publishers.

Edwin Alexander MacDowell (#882), also of Irish descent, was born in New York City in 1861. He studied musical composition overseas at conservatories in France and Germany---with Debussy as a fellow student.

In 1896, Columbia University created a special musical chair for the 35-year-old composer, which he held for eight years. In that period MacDowell composed two piano concertos and many shorter pieces and songs, as well as four major piano sonatas, including the popular *Indian Suite* which incorporated many captivating "native American" melodies.

#882

By the turn of the century, MacDowell's program music, heavily influenced by European romanticism, was considered the high-water mark of serious American musical composition. He died at the age of 47.

#649

In 1903, only months after Samuel Pierpont Langley's experimental "*Aerodrome*" dropped twice into the Potomac from the stern of the world's first aircraft carrier, a pair of Ohio bicycle makers quietly surmounted the gusty onshore winds 60 miles north of Cape Hatteras and put man into powered flight.

Seven years earlier, those skilled mechanics Wilbur and Orville Wright, 29 and 25 years old, had been inspired by Otto Lilienthal's more than 2,000 successful German glider flights, to begin building their own heavier-than-air flying machine.

Organizing their Dayton bicycle repair shop into an airplane factory, the Wright brothers first experimented with an important, patentable leap forward; flight direction controlled by moving areas of the wing assembly, rather than by repositioning the pilot's body. After that major contribution to airplane design, plus exhaustive wind tunnel calculations of pressure, lift, and drag, the Wrights took on the design and construction of a lightweight 12-horsepower four-cylinder gasoline motor, with heavy-duty bicycle chains to drive two propellers on what until then had been only a glider.

By 1903 they were ready. On December 17 on the sand dunes of Kitty Hawk, North Carolina---seven years after Otto Lilienthal died in a glider accident---both Wright brothers made controlled flights in their 600-pound power-driven airplane, landing safely each time. The first flight, by Orville, lasted 12 seconds. The last, 59 seconds by Wilbur, covered 852 feet at almost 10 mph (#C45).

The Wrights returned to Dayton and continued their experiments, building larger and more stable versions (#Q8) of their original "*Flyer A.*" By 1908, they were making (and breaking) flight records all over the United States and Europe. On September 12 Orville remained in the air for over an hour. The Army began purchasing Wright biplanes for military use.

By then Wilbur was deep in patent litigation; he died of typhoid in Dayton in 1912. Angered by Smithsonian Institution support for its Secretary Langley's tortured claim to the first powered flight, Orville refused to donate the brothers' "*Flyer A*" (#649), shipping it instead to London's Kensington Science Museum. It was returned to the United States (and the Smithsonian) in 1948, only after Orville had died.

THREE CENTS

ANNIVERSARYPANAMA

THE WORLD POWER

#802

In the late 18th and early 19th centuries, the expanding United States collected a sizeable number of non-contiguous possessions, either by purchase or peace treaties with their former colonial governments. Such areas later became independent (Philippines) or were officially incorporated into the United States, as territories (Virgin Islands, Guam, American Samoa), commonwealths (Puerto Rico), administrative areas (Canal Zone, Wake Island, Midway Island), trusteeships (Marianas, Carolines, Marshalls), or even states (Alaska, Hawaii). In addition to the states, many of the other areas now enjoy qualified representation in Congress.

The 132-mile-square American Virgin Islands were discovered by Columbus on his second voyage through the Caribbean. St. Thomas was seized by a Danish trading company in 1672; St. John's was claimed eleven years later; and in 1733 the company purchased St. Croix from the French. Twenty-one years later Frederick V made all three islands a Danish royal colony. In 1917, the United States bought the Virgins for $25 million, preventing German U-boats from using their harbors (#802).

The large Caribbean island of Puerto Rico was another 1493 Columbus discovery; the indigenous Arawak population was soon exterminated by Spanish *conquistadores*. In the 16th and 17th centuries Puerto Rico's status as a Spanish colony was unsuccessfully challenged by British and French invaders. Eighteen ninety-eight was perhaps the most important year in the colony's modern history. In February Spain granted Puerto Rico a slight measure of autonomy. In October, the Spanish-American War brought down an American army. Fifteen days before Christmas, Spain agreed to make a present of Puerto Rico to the United States. Initially a U.S. territory, the island became a commonwealth in 1952 (#801). Subsequent agitation for statehood or independence has been undercut by the apparent economic advantages of commonwealth status.

The Pacific Hawaiian Islands, 2,100 miles west of San Francisco, were discovered in 1778 by Captain James Cook. The eight major islands and numerous islets had been settled a thousand

#801

years earlier by adventurous tribesmen sailing from Polynesia. Cook called the group "Sandwich Islands" after his generous patron and First Lord of the Admiralty, John Montagu, earl of Sandwich. The natives paid little attention to the explorer's nomenclature, and later killed him.

For the next hundred years Hawaii, welcoming naval commerce from all over the world, remained independent under native chiefs (#799), but in the last half of the 19th century its economic and political ties to the United States created a strong annexation movement in both the U.S. Congress and the islands. In 1898 the drive finally proved successful, and two years later Hawaii became a territory. World War II cemented relations between the two interdependent entities, and on August 31, 1959, Hawaii became America's 50th state.

❦

Philippines #215

The Philippine Islands, a collection of 7,000 densely populated islands and rocks in the Malay Archipelago, were discovered by Ferdinand Magellan on his trip around the world in 1521. In less than 50 years *conquistadores* and missionaries were consolidating Spanish control. The next three centuries were filled with native revolts for independence, interspersed with long periods of peaceful agricultural development. During the Spanish-American War of 1898, the invading United States troops gave temporary support to the Philippine independence movement, but were soon hunting down its leaders (*Philippines #215*). It took another half century, plus suffering under the Japanese occupation during World War II, before Congress finally granted the Philippines full independence---on July 4, 1946.

❦

The tiny island of Guam in the Western Pacific, inhabited mainly by Chamorro natives, was also discovered by Magellan and colonized by Spain. The 1898 Treaty of Paris, concluding the Spanish-American War, transferred the strategically-located island to the United States (*Guam #2*). In 1917 control of the unincorporated Territory of Guam was given to the Navy Department. In World War II the island was occupied by the Japanese, who were only dislodged after fierce fighting. In 1950 an act of Congress transferred Navy control to the Interior Department; Guamanians became American citizens.

Guam #2

#566

"Keep your ancient lands, your storied pomp!" cries she
With silent lips. "Give me your tired, your poor,
Your huddled masses yearning to breathe free,
The wretched refuse of your teeming shore.
Send these, the homeless, tempest-tost to me,
I lift my lamp beside the golden door!"

In an era of increasing foreign economic hardship, social dissidence, and political unrest, the great copper-clad lady in New York Bay---*Liberty Enlightening the World (#566, 1041)*---spoke thusly in 1883 to the imagination of 34-year-old Emma Lazarus. The closing lines of her famous sonnet, written to support the struggling pedestal fund campaign for Frédéric Auguste Bartholdi's giant statue, were affixed to its base in 1903.

The *"Statue of Liberty"* was a gift to the United States by France to commemorate the centennial of both countries' revolutions. Since 1886, the colossal figure on its granite-faced pedestal, rising more than 300 feet above the waters of New York harbor, has welcomed all foreign visitors, including the tens of millions of European immigrants who swept into the country at the turn of the century. The statue quickly came to symbolize the United States itself.

To northern and western Europeans through the late 1800s, and to even more eastern and southern Europeans after that time, America was a golden "Land of Opportunity" where anyone could build a better life, starting at the lowest rung of the social and economic ladder in mines, mills, factories, and sweatshops.

Such a huge and virtually unchecked foreign flood supplied the inexhaustible pool of cheap, unskilled labor desperately needed for the country's rapidly expanding industrialization. Among many Anglo-Saxon Americans whose grandfathers and great-grandfathers had been immigrants themselves, the new influx of foreigners also stirred xenophobic fears of Catholicism, political radicalism, and "mongrelization."

Such racism somewhat dimmed Emma Lazarus's "lamp beside the golden door." It not only ignored the ideals of the Declaration of Independence, but also failed to grasp how America's rich diversity of ethnic and cultural talent is not a weakness, but an enormous democratic strength.

Spurred by the Civil War, the United States proceeded to transform itself from an agricultural into a major industrial nation. Within 30 years, the change was almost complete. Hundreds of factory towns and cities across the country (#Q9) joined the historic textile mill towns of southern New England.

But many valuable social characteristics of early American life were lost in the inevitable materialism that marked the new rough-and-tumble economy. "Money is no longer under taboo," complained one old-school-tie New Englander, "One's own money and that of one's neighbors is largely talked about...as often in polite conversation as in a tariff debate."

In traditional form the new industrialization demanded unrestrained exploitation of a large labor pool, based on nearby urban centers, with extensive municipal services that created an increasingly complex economy.

Unlike their more independent agricultural brethren, members of the urban working class found themselves relying more and more on the shrinking good will of faceless management and stockholders. Workers took full advantage of their constitutional rights to organize into craft and trade unions, while aggressively pursuing their economic demands through lengthy strikes.

Employers fought back in an often appallingly violent struggle between capital and labor. The enormous industrial production of the United States grew in a see-saw manner, against a continuing background of war, boom, crash, and economic depression.

This push-pull eventually produced our modified capitalist economy, in which the government regularly intervenes to restrain socially unacceptable exploitation of markets or labor.

❧

#1082

In 1882, to celebrate the importance of the workingman, Labor Day (#1082) was established by the Noble Order of the Knights of Labor, precursor of the AFL-CIO and founded by a group of Philadelphia garment workers. At its height before succumbing to factional dispute, the Knights operated a 700,000-member industrial union that welcomed women, African-Americans, and employers, barring only bankers, stockholders, lawyers, and gamblers. In 1894 Congress made Labor Day a national holiday.

In 1878, the man who built the Suez Canal was ready to conquer the Central American isthmus. But after eleven years of poor planning, peculation, and yellow fever, Ferdinand de Lesseps's dream of a sea-level French canal between the Atlantic and Pacific slowly disintegrated into a mass of rusting machinery.

Then followed a tale of "big-stick" diplomacy, as twisted as a jungle vine.

The story begins as far back as 1850, when the U.S. and Great Britain signed a treaty guaranteeing neither country would ever *"exercise any dominion over Nicaragua, the Mosquito coast, Costa Rica, or any part of Central America."* That included digging a canal between the oceans to slice thousands of miles off the sea route around Cape Horn.

Fifty years later Britain relented. By then many Americans wanted to see a Nicaraguan, not a Panamanian canal; they sniffed at the French asking price for the old de Lesseps concesssion.

Enter a Parisian entrepreneur named Philippe Bunau-Varilla. Distributing Nicaraguan stamps to U.S. Congressman that pictured active volcanoes along that potential canal route, he succeeded in switching their votes to Panama, while he got the French to drop the price. The U.S. offered to pay off Colombia (which owned Panama) with $10 million. The Colombians felt insulted; they wanted a far bigger check than that.

So in 1903 Bunau-Varilla led a quick revolt that broke off the piece we now call the Republic of Panama from Colombia. The U.S. contributed a gunboat or two. After such shenanigans, building the actual canal---from 1907 to 1914---was almost an anticlimax. Chief engineer George Washington Goethals copied an idea from the 1666 Canal du Midi, the oldest canal in France. He led water to the highest Panama locks, 85 feet above sea level, from even higher streams flowing off the continental divide.

Teddy Roosevelt (#557) came down and had his picture taken at the controls of a steam shovel. Tens of thousands of West Indian workers finished the job (#856). Seven years later Uncle Sam made a $25 million cash apology to Colombia.

The last time we looked, Panama was still slated to take control of the canal, in 1999.

World War I was the catastrophic conclusion to a deadly struggle by imperial nations for political and economic control of Europe and colonial territories around the world. Diplomatic and military alliances made strange bedfellows out of such *Central Powers* as Germany and Turkey; and out of their opposing *"Allies,"* such as Russia, the United States, and Japan.

The assassination of an Austro-Hungarian archduke by a Balkan nationalist became Germany's excuse for declaring war on Russia on August 1, 1914. Nation after nation, feeding on years of *revanchist* and militarist propaganda, was quickly drawn into the bloody conflict.

This war on many fronts lasted 1,564 days. It took more than ten million lives. In an attempt to break the long stalemate of terrifying trench warfare---poison gas and tanks were introduced. Thousands of soldiers were slaughtered in the name of various fatherlands and motherlands, for advances of only a few thousand yards. The murderous machine gun, mainly used against native populations on other continents, was now turned against the youth of Europe and Britain with devastating effect.

The isolationist United States remained clear of the carnage for more than 31 months. But several billion dollars of unsecured loans to the beleaguered Allies, exacerbated by Germany's declaration of unrestricted submarine warfare (triggered by an effective British blockade), finally brought the U.S., with its comparatively unlimited industrial and manpower resources, into the war. By the end of 1917 more than a million American troops *(#2154)* under General John Joseph Pershing *(#1042A)* were in France. In his 1931 autobiography, Pershing denied ever having said "anything so splendid" as *"Lafayette, we are here!"*; he blamed that on his chief disbursing officer.

Popular revolutions eventually broke out in Russia and Germany. Entire divisions of French troops mutinied. The Central Powers suddenly faced unexpected political and economic problems, and moved swiftly to cut their losses. The struggle ended on November 11, 1918, when an exhausted German government finally signed an armistice.

Within four months the United States issued a stamp to celebrate the Allied victory *(#537)*. Sixteen months of fighting left the U.S. with 320,710 casualties, including 117,000 dead.

4¢

LO

G MAY IT WAVE

S OF AMERICA

BETWEEN TWO WARS

On the morning of May 15, 1918, while almost a million American doughboys were still slogging through the mud of northern France, mechanics on an improvised Washington, D.C. airstrip were gassing up a brand-new Curtiss JN-4H, one of the famous 93-mph World War I "*Jenny*" trainers. Postmaster General Albert S. Burleson had decided America was ready for airmail service between the nation's capital and New York City, with a stop in Philadelphia. Postage would be 24¢ an ounce, 10¢ special delivery service included.

At the controls of America's first airmail plane was George Boyle, an inexperienced Air Force lieutenant and future son-in-law of the chairman of the influential Interstate Commerce Commission. President Wilson came over from the White House to see Boyle take off---in the wrong direction. An hour later the lieutenant phoned in from Maryland. He had crashed, flipping his *Jenny* upside down. The airmail bag was retrieved for another try; an alternate suggestion to use a train was rejected.

On May 14th, the day before that historic flight, William Thomas Robey, a stamp-collecting Washington brokerage clerk, bought a sheet of 100 of the new red-and-blue stamps (#C3). To his amazement and delight, all the *Jennys* were flying upside down (#C3a); a hurried pressman had inverted at least one red sheet while printing his blue plate. When Robey asked to see more of the 24¢ airmail stock, the stamp clerk slammed the window in his face. Later two postal inspectors tried to buy back Robey's unique sheet (for $24); he faced them down. Five days later Robey sold the sheet for $15,000. Since then, a single "inverted *Jenny*" stamp has fetched a quarter of a million dollars.

Right side up or upside down, airmail service boomed. In two months, postal volume dropped the rate to 16¢. By the end of the first year the mandatory 10¢ delivery charge was removed.

Two years later, in peacetime, the government inaugurated a 33-1/2-hour transcontinental mail-by-air route between New York and San Francisco. The planes flew only by daylight; at night the mailbags were transferred to express trains.

Finally, on July 1, 1924, with illuminated beacons twinkling all along the Rockies/Sierras route (#C11), day-or-night transcontinental airmail service---New York-Chicago-Cheyenne-San Francisco---became a reality (#C9).

#855

In 1778, George Ewing wrote in his Valley Forge diary about "playing at base" in the snow with other Continental soldiers. Nine years later the faculty at Princeton forbade students "to play with balls and sticks in the back common of the college." The game of baseball that slowly evolved from such modest beginnings is not much different from the 18th century children's games of *one old cat*, *two old cat*, *three old cat*, and *four old cat*. All are team sports that reward individualism.

But 20-year-old Abner Doubleday, later a famous Union Civil War hero, is supposed to have invented America's "national game" from scratch---for military cadets at Cooperstown, New York, in 1839 (#855). So let's give Abner a perfunctory tip of the hat, and move on to some of baseball's other major contributors:

Like the early player who suggested that the runner be *tagged* with the ball---instead of throwing it at his head.

Or Alexander Cartwright, whose inspiration in placing bases exactly 90 feet apart creates split-second plays.

Or Henry Chadwick, who in 1858 felt compelled to write down baseball's rules and specifications. With revisions, of course, Chadwick's notebook has governed the national pastime since.

Both Union and Confederate soldiers played baseball for camp diversion during the Civil War---but never in opposing leagues. Skipping over several interim "Associations," league contests had to wait for the National League, founded a decade after the war, and the American League, founded in 1900. The first "world's championship series" between those two groups was played three years later. Little since, including wars or earthquakes, has been able to interrupt that annual meeting.

The advent of television created sweeping changes in baseball's public audience. Except for important in-season rivalries, season finales, and the leagues' "Series," most baseball stadiums are not exactly full at game time, with tens of millions of fans following the play in living rooms and bars.

A few of baseball's outstanding heroes, including Babe Ruth (#2046), Jackie Robinson, and Roberto Clemente have been honored on United States postage stamps. Like *four old cat* before it, American baseball fever can be catching; the game is now also played in Canada, Cuba, Italy, Japan, Mexico, Puerto Rico, the Soviet Union, and Taiwan.

The greatest comedians are those who can make you laugh at yourself. William Penn Adair Rogers (#975), born in Oklahoma Indian Territory in 1879, filled the bill.

#975

After spending his earliest years on the plains as a lasso-twirling, joke-cracking cowpuncher, Will Rogers entered vaudeville, using his actual persona; by 1915 he was a big star on Broadway. Rogers exercised his sly, gently mocking "frontier wit" on Americans for more than two decades---as a syndicated newspaper columnist and author, as well as an actor in stage musicals, radio, and motion pictures.

In Will Rogers's time there were no vast audiences waiting to be automatically captured by nightly television monologists. But his easy homespun humor soon won over the country---in the great American political and social comedic tradition of writer-lecturers like the fervent abolitionist David Ross Locke ("Petroleum Vesuvius Nasby"), the indigenist Charles Farrar Browne ("Artemus Ward"), and the anti-imperialist Finley Peter Dunne ("Mr. Dooley").

Like those three (and Mark Twain), Will Rogers held the mirror up to U.S. nature---with telling effect. "All I know," he recited in his distinctive Oklahoma twang, "is what I read in the papers"---adding, "all Politics is Apple Sauce."

Rogers disarmed critical readers and listeners with his comment, "I never met a man I didn't like." Then he became one of the country's best-loved (and highest-paid) performers by hilariously skewering every boob in America.

The $14 billion stock crash of 1929 provided Rogers with a mother lode of caustic observation. As the Great Depression advanced, he warned radio audiences that the United States would be "the first starving nation in the world to go to the poorhouse in an automobile. If our 'big men' can't get the country back to work," he added, "they just ain't big men."

An indefatigable air traveler, Rogers flew wherever he could. In 1935 he was touring Alaska with solo-round-the-world record holder and fellow Oklahoman Wiley Post. As they took off from Point Barrow, their float plane flipped over onto its back. Both men were killed.

The State of Oklahoma honored America's "cowboy philosopher" with a bronze statue and a shrine.

#2089, #2046

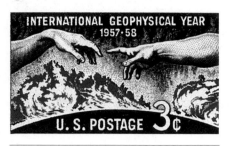

By the 1930s few areas of the world were left to explore, by the United States or anyone else. The inhospitable Antarctic, world's fifth largest continent, 3,300 miles across and far bigger than the U.S., represented a last chunk of *terra incognita*.

Tossing about in ice-choked Antarctic waters back in 1773, world circumnavigator James Cook suspected the existence of this giant continental land mass. Sealing and whaling captains from many nations were soon exploring its icy edges. In 1839 a four-ship expedition led by U.S. Navy Commander Charles Wilkes sailed 1,500 miles along the Antarctic coast.

By the end of the 19th century, with North Polar areas mainly explored, the South Pole beckoned to adventurers of many nations. In 1911 the Norwegian explorer Roald Amundsen beat Royal Navy Commander Robert Falcon Scott to the South Pole by only a few days; Scott's five-man British expedition perished miserably during its return to base.

With the South Pole conquered on foot, it was left to an experienced U.S. Navy aviator, 41-year-old Lieutenant Commander Richard Evelyn Byrd, to establish an airbase---"*Little America*"---on the Ross ice shelf, whence he could fly above the Pole. On November 29, 1929, Byrd and three companions completed that 1,600-mile round trip. The world cheered; Congress made Byrd a rear admiral, retired.

Four years later Byrd led a second U.S. expedition to explore, mainly by air, an additional half million square miles of the continent (*#733*). Byrd himself spent a -83°F. winter alone in a weather station hut near the Pole, barely surviving the effects of carbon monoxide fumes from a faulty stove.

The culmination of all 20th century Antarctic exploration was the International Geophysical Year---July 1957 to December 1958---during which time scientists from a dozen nations conducted ambitious Antarctic research programs in oceanography, meteorology, seismology, glaciology, geomagnetism, cosmic rays, ionospheric phenomena, and aurora glow (*#1107*).

The next year, in an unprecedented gesture of scientific cooperation, all countries participating in the I.G.Y. signed a special treaty temporarily suspending territorial claims to Antarctica, and setting the continent aside for further research.

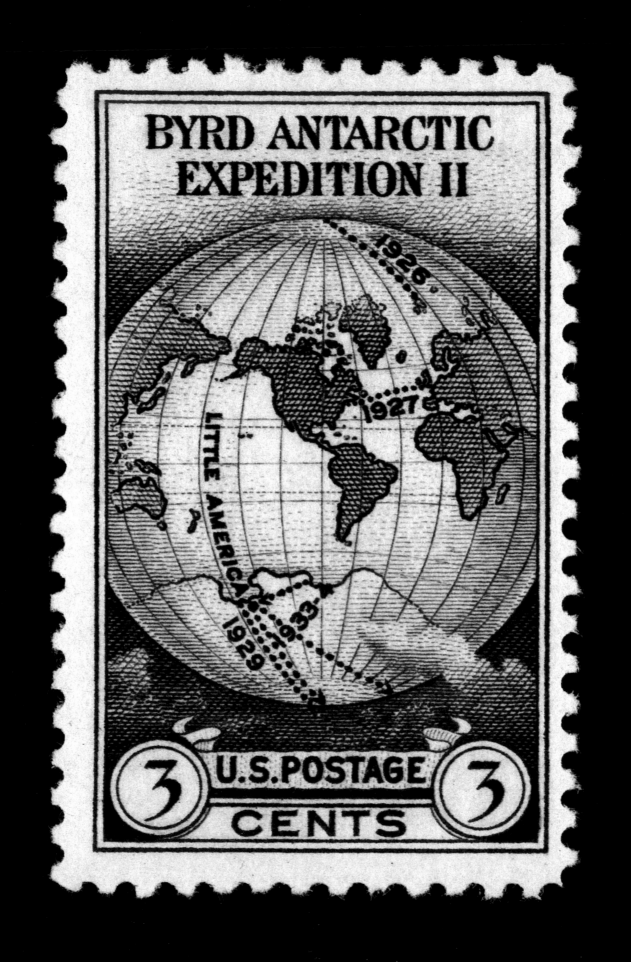

BOULDER DAM·1935

3¢ 3¢

U.S. POSTAGE

#728

The United States's first blockbuster international exhibition and trade fair (following the relatively sedate 1876 Philadelphia Centennial Exposition) was Chicago's World's Columbian Exposition in 1893. The fair was a year late in heralding the 400th anniversary of the arrival of the Genoese navigator, but its grandiose "White City" structures set an architectural style that subsequent U.S. fairs would strive to surpass. Like most American fairs, the Chicago Exposition was built on undeveloped, reclaimed land.

Eight years later, the Pan-American Exposition in Buffalo's Delaware Park successfully copied Chicago's classical style, with widespread use of electric lighting. For the seven-months-long St. Louis Exposition in 1904 to celebrate the 100th anniversary of the Louisiana Purchase, 1,240 acres of gardens, lagoons, fountains, and sculpture were created to set off a handsomely designed group of pavilions.

By 1915, American fair planning and design had become a major architectural sideline and showcase. That year's Panama-Pacific Exposition on the shores of San Francisco Bay sheltered visitors to its various international exhibits within a series of striking courts, embellished with floodlit, colorful plaster decorations. A fair in San Diego the same year stressed that city's heritage, with Spanish motifs.

By 1933 it was again Chicago's turn, with the theme exposition *A Century of Progress* to celebrate the 100th anniversary of the construction of Fort Dearborn and the city's birth (#728). These were modern times; previous architectural concepts were cast aside, and the fair's functional buildings, again placed on the shore of Lake Michigan, quickly routed 22 million visitors easily through the many scientific and industrial exhibits.

Expositions in San Diego, Dallas, and Cleveland between 1935 and 1937 were merely curtain raisers to the two spectacular fairs of 1939-40: the palatial exhibition halls of the 16-million-visitor Golden Gate International Exhibition on an island in San Francisco Bay (#852), and the incredible vision of the future projected by the 55-million-visitor New York World's Fair, symbolized forever by its striking Trylon/Perisphere combination (#853). Both fairs were resplendent foretastes of a bright new world, soon to be swallowed up in the horrors of World War II.

#852

WORLD WAR II AND AFTER

Franklin Delano Roosevelt---"*FDR*"---was 39 years old when disaster struck. Poliomyelitis wasted his legs. He would never again walk unassisted. In the days before television, a kinder, gentler media helped keep that fact a secret, but FDR's promising political career lay in shambles: he had served as Assistant Secretary of the Navy in 1913, and run (unsuccessfully) for Vice-President in 1920.

Years of physical rehabilitation with devoted family support allowed FDR to rise above his tremendous handicap---and serve two terms as reform governor of New York State. But the governor's office was merely a springboard for a man whose energies always equalled his ambitions. When the Democratic Party horsetraded nominees for the 1932 presidential election, it chose FDR. He subsequently won the presidency hands down.

Few leaders of the United States ever faced a more challenging crisis. The country was at low ebb. Stock values had collapsed. The unemployed were selling apples on the street. World War I veterans camping out in Washington parks stormed the steps of the Capitol---only General MacArthur's tanks and tear gas kept them from occupying Congress.

FDR used radio "fireside chats" to revitalize the nation's attention, and generate public support for a host of "*New Deal*" programs (*#732*). He pressured a nervous Congress to grant him emergency powers, threatening to "pack" the Supreme Court when its judges challenged his new legislation.

As FDR expanded government economic controls, he introduced unprecedented deficit financing, welfare relief, public works programs (*#774*), and new taxes. With an eye on the rise of totalitarianism, he maneuvered the United States into fuller participation in international affairs. After the outbreak of war in Europe, he generously assisted the allies.

Pearl Harbor carried the United States into the war. For three and a half years FDR presided over U.S. participation in World War II (*#905*), flying around the globe, visiting allied heads of state, and coordinating wartime planning and postwar reconstruction---enunciated by his "Four Freedoms" (*#933*).

In the spring of 1945, less than a month before the Nazi surrender, a worn-out FDR died. He had won an unprecedented four presidential elections. He was only 63 years old.

#905

CHURCHILL

U.S. 5 CENTS

#1264

For almost a decade, the Germans openly armed for another attempt at conquering Europe and the world. The war began on September 1, 1939, with a "*blitzkrieg*," a lightning offensive into Poland. Neutralized by a Nazi "non-aggression" pact, the Soviets swiftly gobbled up their own share of that unhappy country.

Then came a half year of what some cynics called a "phony war," followed in the spring of 1940 by the Nazi invasion of Denmark, Norway, the Low Countries, and northern France. The British expeditionary army in Europe quickly pulled back to the Channel, and was evacuated in the "Miracle of Dunkirk." At Cap Gris-Nez, the Germans were only 21 miles from England.

As the French retreated southward, Mussolini and the Italians struck at southern France. Roosevelt quickly pledged "all material resources of the United States" to aid the Western allies. Most Americans were eager to stay out of another world war, but they instinctively feared the spread of totalitarianism. Under an umbrella of neutrality, they generally supported delicate Administration "lend-lease" commitments to exchange over-age U.S. destroyers and other essential armaments for superannuated British naval bases in the Western Hemisphere.

The ability of the British people, led by a charismatic prime minister, Winston Churchill (*#1264*), to survive the Nazi onslaught was balanced at knife edge. In October 1940 Roosevelt, in a pre-third-term campaign speech, assured American parents: "*Your boys are not going to be sent into any foreign wars.*" But as he spoke, U.S. industrial power was slowly being hammered into an "arsenal of democracy."

The war took an unexpected turn in June 1941. Along a thousand-mile front, 164 Nazi and satellite divisions launched a devastating attack on the "non-aggressor" U.S.S.R. Their invasion automatically created a new anti-Axis partner. After half a year, when it became clear that the Soviets were holding their own against the Germans, the United States extended lend-lease. "*Without the miracle of American production,*" Stalin acknowledged, "*we could never have fought the war.*" By the winter of 1941-42, the German offensive was blunted.

Japan, an Axis power since September 1940, chose that now-or-never moment to try to sink 94 U.S. Navy ships lined up like sitting ducks in Pearl Harbor.

#1393

The European war against the Axis was fought on three fronts---east, west, and south---with valuable assistance from underground movements in the occupied countries. Allied strategy called for surface assaults along a wide perimeter in the direction of Berlin, accompanied by heavy aerial bombardment.

In June 1942 General Dwight D. Eisenhower (*#1393*), the U.S. Army's chief of operations, was selected as supreme allied commander in Europe. In November, U.S. forces (*#1067, 1013*) landed in Algeria to join "Free French" troops under General Charles de Gaulle. The British successfully blocked Rommel's drive towards Cairo. By May of the following year, bitter fighting had driven the Germans out of North Africa.

Sicily was conquered that summer, and Italy was invaded. Despite the surrender of the Italian army in September, continued German resistance made the campaign for Northern Italy long and costly. The allies entered Rome only after almost a year of bloody "leap-frog" coastal landings.

Only two days after the capture of Rome, France was invaded by the Allies along a line of northwestern beachheads, with another landing two months later on the Mediterranean coast. Heavy pressure from both east and west compelled a general Nazi retreat. The liberation of Paris in August was celebrated by a grand military parade; the GIs (*#934, 1017*) who marched down the Champs Élysées continued straight out of Paris towards the Rhine. At the end of the year, an unexpected German counterattack under bitter winter conditions in the Belgian Ardennes region caused 77,000 allied casualties. As flying weather improved, the German advance was crushed.

That *Battle of the Bulge* was the Wehrmacht's last offensive gasp. Allied units led by General George S. Patton, Jr. (*#1026*) crossed the Rhine early in March, while the Soviet Army swept around Berlin. The Russians and Americans met at the Elbe River at the end of April. Hitler shot himself in his Berlin bunker. His body, doused in gasoline, was burned by devoted aides.

After only 13 years, the *Thousand Year Reich* was destroyed, but at terrible cost. Almost 200,000 American GIs died in Europe; their fellow soldiers liberated horrifying Nazi extermination factories, in which 6,000,000 Jews and hundreds of thousands of other Europeans were starved or gassed to death.

#934

#1026

3¢

GEORGE S. PATTON, JR.

CES OF THE U. S. ARMY

DOUGLAS MacARTHUR

#1424

Pearl Harbor plunged the United States into World War II. It took many months, while Japanese forces spread across Southeast Asia, to assemble an adequate U.S. military response. The enemy attack on Hawaii was followed by their capture of several strategic South Pacific islands. General Douglas MacArthur (#1424), recalled from retirement a few months earlier to command U.S. forces in the Far East, was evacuated to Australia. American soldiers trapped in Manila Bay's Fort Corregidor (#925) were cruelly marched off to Bataan prison camps.

The bad news from the Pacific eventually became good. In May 1942 an invasion threat to New Guinea was smashed in the Battle of the Coral Sea; for the first time in naval history, a sea battle was fought exclusively by carrier-based aircraft.

A month later 169 Japanese war vessels, with 700 planes and 21 submarines, challenged a smaller U.S. force off Midway Island. A deciphered Japanese naval code aided American strategy; a quarter of the enemy fleet was destroyed. Japan's eastward advance was blocked. Any invasion threat to Hawaii and the U. S. West Coast evaporated.

In the last five months of 1942, Japanese naval and ground forces on Guadalcanal in the Solomons were severely battered, and withdrew. Other actions soon transformed the war into a roll-up operation, as islands were seized and turned into "unsinkable aircraft carriers." Japan went on the defensive.

Amphibious assaults swept closer and closer to Tokyo as U.S. naval aircraft continued to punish the Japanese fleet. On June 19, 1944, in the "Marianas Turkey Shoot," the enemy lost 315 planes; the Americans only 23. A month later reoccupation of the Marianas permitted B-29 bombers to strike at Tokyo.

In October General MacArthur's return to the Philippines precipitated the greatest naval battle of the war: Leyte Gulf became another Japanese disaster.

A volcanic islet 800 miles from Tokyo held two airstrips that could support U.S. fighter cover for the B-29s. On February 15, 1945, U.S. Marines invaded the island. After four weeks of savage fighting the enemy was finally dislodged---90% were killed. In the great symbolic act of the Pacific war, six marines raised the American flag over Iwo Jima (#929).

For Japan, the end was near.

UNITED STATES OF AMERICA

CORREGIDOR

3¢ POSTAGE

#925

#929

#1067

#1013

Harry S. Truman

U.S. Postage 8 cents

#1499

Harry S. Truman (#1499) of Independence, Missouri, and The White House, Washington, D.C., was the closest thing to an American mainstream president during the 20th century. The first career of this piano-playing "Man from Independence" was haberdashery. He soon switched to law, and entered local midwestern politics.

The subsequent 12-year rise of the unaffected, supremely self-confident World War I artillery captain through the corrupt wards and districts of Kansas City, culminated in 1934 in his election to the United States Senate.

Ten years later, despite serious political differences with the New Deal administration, Truman's record was sufficiently middle-of-the-road for him to be offered the vice-presidency of Roosevelt's fourth term. On the President's death on April 12, 1945, Truman shouldered the awesome burden of defining the role of the United States in the chaotic postwar world.

He quickly approved the world's first use of nuclear weapons against the faltering Japanese, giving rise to a military *vs.* humanitarian controversy that will never be resolved; discontinued the U.S. wartime rapprochement with the Soviets; and hardened our opposition to left-wing governments everywhere.

Instead of retreating to the traditional political isolationism of the Midwest, Truman moved aggressively to assist the economic and military recovery of what quickly became known, after Churchill's 1946 "iron curtain" speech in Fulton, Missouri, as the *Free World*.

To reestablish European stability while wearing down Soviet resolve, the "Truman Doctrine," the "Marshall Plan," the West Berlin airlift, and the formation of the North Atlantic Treaty Organization (#1008) quickly established a political pattern that dominated East-West relations for almost half a century. Despite minor corruption that rocked his administration, in an atmosphere of growing political conformity that opened the door to McCarthyism, Truman compiled a reasonable record of social and economic reform.

In 1948, to the surprise of almost everyone except Harry S. Truman, and despite a three-way Democratic Party split, the president was elected to succeed himself.

#928

Milestones along the often illusory path to world peace and security through international cooperation have included the International Telegraphic Union (1865), the Red Cross (1864), the Universal Postal Union (1874), the Hague Peace Conferences (1899 and 1907), and the Permanent Court of Arbitration (1899). Andrew Carnegie's "peace palace" built at the Hague is still used by the International Court of Justice.

The concept of a "league" of nations was first broached to the United States Congress and the American people in a speech by Woodrow Wilson in the spring of 1917. Two years later, the Versailles Conference incorporated it in the treaty ending World War I, but the U.S. Senate declined League membership.

The League of Nations quickly found it difficult to take action against its more powerful members. For two decades it struggled with little success to achieve the purposes for which it had been established. Although the League forcefully expelled the Soviet Union in 1939 for invading Finland, it proved powerless to halt the spread of international fascism. The result was World War II.

The Allies, dubbed the "*United Nations*" by Franklin Delano Roosevelt in 1941, quickly recognized the need for a new and more powerful international organization to help maintain peace and security in the postwar world. A joint declaration to that purpose was issued in Moscow in 1943 by the United States, the Soviet Union, Great Britain, and China. The founding conference of the new organization was held at San Francisco on April 25, 1945 (#928), attended by 51 member nations.

In the dissension-filled decades that followed, marked by local "police actions," invasions, and full-fledged wars, the United Nations served as both cockpit and conference table. Like its crippled predecessor the League of Nations, the U.N. has suffered from member abuse. Its best record has been established in areas of human welfare.

For ten years Eleanor Roosevelt (*#2105)* served as United States delegate to the U.N., winning over her earlier critics with unusual vigor and charm. In 1946 she became chairperson of the U.N.'s International Commission on Human Rights. Her tireless dedication to humanitarian causes brought the late President's wife worldwide recognition and enormous respect.

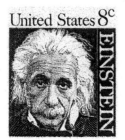

#1285

On the afternoon of December 2, 1942, as the Allies consolidated their invasion of North Africa and continued to inch forward against the Japanese in the Pacific, a small group of atomic scientists in Chicago presided over the first man-made nuclear chain reaction.

They gathered around a neat pile of uranium and graphite blocks in a converted squash court under the stands of the University of Chicago's Stagg Field. At 3:25 pm Enrico Fermi confirmed that the nuclear reaction was indeed self-sustaining. Albert Einstein's (#1285) most famous equation, $E=mc^2$, had been put to work.

From a *military* point of view, the age of controlled nuclear fission ushered in that Monday afternoon in 1942 eventually led the U.S. into an escalating arms race with the U.S.S.R., with each nation scrambling to assure its population they would never suffer the fate of the Japanese civilians at Hiroshima and Nagasaki. The dire competition soon engendered a proliferation of intercontinental and shorter-range atomic missiles, with delivery systems of increasing complexity.

Before long both nations were "atomically overbuilt," with sufficient weaponry to destroy each other many times over. Recent bilateral nuclear arms reduction agreements offer a major hope of rational correction.

From the *civilian* point of view, the development of atomic fission for non-military uses has also been clouded. The complicated technology for generating atomic power, originally promised under the rubric *"Atoms for Peace"* (#1070) to be so cheap it would almost be free, has actually created a great increase in U.S. electric rates.

Hanging above us all for almost half a century has been the specter of insidious or catastrophic nuclear radiation. Many early atomic reactors have been likened to loaded pistols---in the case of Three Mile Island, the safety catch almost slipped off. At Chernobyl it did.

One hopes that historians decades hence will be able to record that such near disasters led the United States, at least, to tighter controls, increased safety precautions, and a rational method of atomic waste disposal.

That would indeed be the dawn of a new Nuclear Age.

With the exception of disruptive British incursions during the War of 1812, and minor unpleasantnesses along the Mexican border in 1846 and 1916, United States soil has never trembled beneath the boots of an invading army. But hundreds of thousands of U.S. soldiers have been carried all over the world to defend cherished American concepts of political freedom.

Two major engagements for our troops during the last half of the 20th century were the U.N. police action in Korea, and the war between North and South Vietnam (a conflict previously abandoned by the French). In neither case did U.S. intervention do much to remake Asia in our traditional democratic image.

Five years after the end of World War II and Korea's liberation from the Japanese, and one year after the withdrawal of all U.S. occupation troops, the communist northern half of Korea invaded the non-communist southern half. Forces (mainly American) provided by the United Nations slowly pushed the North Koreans back across the 38th parallel.

General MacArthur's subsequent drive to the Chinese border at the Yalu River (#2152) brought a Chinese army into the action, and might have precipitated World War III had not President Truman quickly replaced the 71-year-old general.

The conflict in Korea inspired the cynical and immensely popular television comedy "M*A*S*H." During years of cease-fire negotiations, it also gave the North Koreans an excuse to construct an incredibly rigid garrison state. South Korea ended up with a flawed democratic government---ignoring many ideals for which American soldiers gave their lives.

Our costly intervention in Vietnam led nowhere. From the insertion of military advisors during the late 1950s to our final troop withdrawal in 1975, through two Democratic and three Republican administrations, the United States suffered almost a quarter-million casualties in Vietnam, creating unparalleled dissidence at home. After our longest war, shabby government treatment of returned veterans produced additional resentment.

Architect Maya Ying Lin's moving Vietnam Memorial in Washington (#2109) is unique in the history of warfare. On its black granite slabs, a finger can trace the names of every one of the 58,174 American soldiers who died in Vietnam.

The feeling of loss is overwhelming.

Vietnam Veterans Memorial USA 20c

#2109

Veterans Korea

USA 22

The United States has always had its sad share of sociopaths and hired killers to prey on its leaders. Since 1864, one out of every seven U.S. presidents has been assassinated in office. Unsuccessful murder attempts were also made on the lives of Theodore Roosevelt, Franklin D. Roosevelt, Gerald Ford, and Ronald Reagan.

While riding with the Governor of Texas through downtown Dallas on November 22, 1963, John Fitzgerald Kennedy (#1287), 35th president of the United States, was killed by a high-powered rifle bullet apparently fired from the upper story of a building along the motorcade route.

The accused assassin was quickly apprehended, but was himself killed by a Dallas nightclub owner before he could be interrogated. Ten months after Kennedy's assassination, a special commission of inquiry headed by Supreme Court Chief Justice Earl Warren established that the killer, Lee Harvey Oswald, had acted alone.

Kennedy, who took office at the age of 43, was able to serve only a thousand days. After three months as president, he saw a long-planned U.S. invasion of Cuba fall apart at the Bay of Pigs. A year and a half later he challenged Nikita Khrushchev "eyeball-to-eyeball," and forced the removal of Soviet missiles from the Caribbean island. Kennedy backed many domestic social programs; gave assistance through his brother Robert (his Attorney General) to the southern civil rights movement; and initiated the ambitious U.S. exploration of space.

The Reverend Martin Luther King, Jr. (#1771), a firm believer in non-violent action for civil rights, led the southern struggle against racial discrimination in the 50s and 60s. He was 39 years old when he was assassinated by James Earl Ray in Memphis on April 4, 1968. Eighteen years later this monumental leader's birthday was declared a national legal public holiday.

Two months after Dr. King's death, Robert F. Kennedy (#1770), then serving as a U.S. Senator from New York, was assassinated by Sirhan Bishara Sirhan while entering a Los Angeles hotel ballroom. Kennedy was 42 years old and had just won the California Democratic nomination for President.

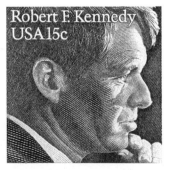

United States & Canada

Peace Bridge 1927-77

USA 13c

OBSERVATORY

INTO SPACE

#966

After World War II, American and Soviet scientists followed similar paths, experimenting with captured 12-ton Nazi *V-2's*, firing them up into the atmosphere (#976), and, based on the test results, designing new, improved rockets. In 1949 a *WAC Corporal* mounted atop a *V-2* sailed 250 miles high over White Sands, New Mexico---and the race was on in earnest.

It was also a race for newspaper space. From 1957 on, international headlines trumpeted every new triumph, as the United States and the U.S.S.R. played catch-up rocketry.

The Soviets were first with two *Sputniks*. The first circled the earth for 23 days, 558 miles up. The second, weighing half a ton, sailed twice as high, carrying a dog named Laika to test the effects of weightlessness on potential human pilots.

The United States caught up early in 1958 with *Explorer I,* which also discovered the Van Allen radiation belts. The next year the Soviets sent *Lunik III* to the far side of the moon. Within half a decade, the international space competitors had launched more than 100 artificial satellites and probes, including orbiting U.S. weather stations like *Tiros I*.

On April 12, 1961, 27-year-old Yuri Alekseyevich Gagarin became the first human to enter space, circling the earth for an hour and a half 188 miles up in the 5-ton Soviet *Vostok*. Less than a month later, 38-year-old Alan Bartlett Shepard, Jr., riding 115 miles high in *Freedom 7*, rocketed 302 miles in 15 minutes to become the first American to cross the space frontier. In August 1961, 26-year-old Gherman Stepanovich Titov demonstrated that man can withstand prolonged weightlessness in space; he made a 17-orbit flight in *Vostok II*, traveling 435,000 miles around the earth in only 25 hours.

Astronauts and cosmonauts now vied with each other to set new records for manned space flight. The first American to enter orbit, on February 20, 1962, was 40-year-old John Herschel Glenn, Jr., in Project Mercury's (#1193) *Friendship 7*---blasting off from Cape Canaveral and traveling three times around the earth in five hours, 188 miles up, splashing down in the Bahamas.

Glenn was followed three months later by 32-year-old Malcolm Scott Carpenter in *Aurora 7* in a second three-orbit flight. By then, the United States was drawing up plans to "put a man on the moon by 1969."

#976

#1193

MERCURY.

#1371

"*In spite of the opinions of certain narrow-minded people who would shut up the human race upon this globe, we shall one day travel to the moon, the planets, and the stars with the same facility, rapidity, and certainty as we now make the ocean voyage from Liverpool to New York!*"

---JULES VERNE *from Earth, 1865*

The Chinese inventor of the first rocket in 1225 A.D. never dreamed his device would one day put men on the Moon.

In the 1860s, the French science-fiction author Jules Verne wrote his arresting *From the Earth to the Moon*, and its even more exciting sequel, *A Trip Around It*. In those two rational works, Verne conceived of an aluminum capsule containing three space travelers, fired from a 900-foot-long cannon at a velocity of 12,000 yards a second, out around the Moon and back.

Although Verne traveled in his imagination, it seemed only a matter of time before scientists would work out the elegant ballistics required to explore this last frontier (*#1371*). Fire a capsule fast enough and it would neatly balance the earth's gravitational pull, and float in space. An extra push, and it would sail off, swing around the Moon, and splash down in the Pacific!

It was no coincidence that Verne's fictional Gun Club president Impey Barbicane and his party blasted off from a point less than 100 miles from today's Kennedy Space Center. Verne understood the required latitude.

"*That's one small step for man... one giant leap for mankind.*"

---NEIL A. ARMSTRONG *from the Moon, 1969*

From July 16 through July 24, 1969, an Apollo spacecraft carrying astronauts Edwin E. "Buzz" Aldrin, Jr., Neil A. Armstrong, and Michael Collins sailed half a million miles on a spectacular trip around the Moon. Undisputed high point of the voyage was a 21-1/2 hour stopover on the Moon's surface (*#C76*) by Aldrin and Armstrong, while Collins orbited overhead.

Those first men on the Moon unfurled a rigid American flag (there is never a breeze), hopped lightly about (there is less gravity), posed for TV, and collected 50 pounds of rock samples for geologists back home. Jules Verne would have rejoiced.

Between 1962, when a retrofire error caused Scott Carpenter to overshoot his landing zone by 250 miles, and 1969, when Neil A. Armstrong and Edwin E. Aldrin, Jr., became the first men to walk on the moon, the United States launched no fewer than 15 successful manned space missions.

There was one calamity at the Kennedy Space Center (foreshadowing the *Challenger* disaster). In January 1967 a flash fire in the control module of *Apollo I* killed the three astronauts--- Virgil I. Grissom, Edward H. White, and Roger B. Chaffee.

In that same 1962-69 period, the Soviets mounted ten missions---with a re-entry disaster of their own. Meanwhile, dozens of unmanned craft were continually lofted from both countries for various scientific and military purposes. Tiny television cameras were even sent to the nearest planets and beyond.

Although the pictures they returned were spectacular, by far the most dramatic events of the entire international space program were those six American landings on the moon in the four years from 1969 to 1972. The landings involved 18 astronauts, and almost made the trip to the moon and back look like the sort of easy commute Jules Verne had dreamed about more than a century earlier.

There were also space shots by U.S. and U.S.S.R. astronauts/cosmonauts to their own "space stations" previously placed in orbit, with extended stays aboard (#1529). It was only a matter of time before the two countries demonstrated a willingness to drop their international rivalry long enough to attempt a joint space effort. The program called for a space vehicle from each nation to link up, in orbit.

That historic scientific and political event took place in July 1975. Vance Brand, Thomas P. Stafford, and Donald K. "Deke" Slayton nudged their *Apollo 18* into position behind *Soyuz 19* (#1569), with Alexei Leonov and Valeri Kubasov aboard. In turn, the spacemen visited each others' spacecraft, and held a joint televised press conference in space.

In a real sense, that link-up acknowledged that despite unresolved ideological differences, we are *all* astronauts and cosmonauts, whirling our way through the ether at more than a thousand miles a minute as fellow passengers on the same planet.

US 10c

APOLLO SOYUZ 1975

PHILATELIC REFERENCE

We gratefully acknowledge the assistance of the Bureau of Engraving and Printing, U.S. Treasury Department; the Philatelic Department, U.S. Postal Service; the Scott Publishing Co.; and the American Philatelic Society's Director of Library Services, Ms. Gini Horn, in helping to compile this descriptive catalog

Scott	Denomination	Designer	Issued	Subject	Source
#24	1¢	Toppan, Carpenter, Casilear & Company	1857	Benjamin Franklin	From a bust by Caffieri
#73p	2¢	National Bank Note Company	1863	Andrew Jackson	From a miniature by Minor K. Kellogg
#114	3¢	National Bank Note Company	1869	Locomotive	---
#120	24¢	National Bank Note Company	1869	Declaration of Independence	From a painting by John Trumbull
#220	2¢	American Bank Note Company	1890	George Washington	From a bust by Jean Antoine Houdon
#229	90¢	Bureau of Engraving and Printing	1895	Commodore Oliver Hazard Perry	From a bust by Wolcott
#230	1¢	American Bank Note Company	1893	Columbus Sights Land	From a painting by William H. Powell
#231	2¢	American Bank Note Company	1893	Landing of Columbus	From a painting by John Vanderlyn
#232	3¢	American Bank Note Company	1893	"Santa Maria"	From a Spanish engraving
#245	$5.00	American Bank Note Company	1893	Portrait of Columbus	From a Spanish medallion
#255	5¢	Bureau of Engraving and Printing	1894	Ulysses S. Grant	From a photograph
#285	1¢	Raymond Ostrander Smith	1898	Marquette on the Mississippi	From a painting by William Lamprecht
#287	4¢	Raymond Ostrander Smith	1898	Indian Hunting Buffalo	From an engraving by Capt. S. Eastman
#293	$2.00	Raymond Ostrander Smith	1898	Mississippi River Bridge at St. Louis	From a ticket to the 1896 Republican National Convention
#296a	4¢	Raymond Ostrander Smith	1901	Electric Automobile	From a photograph of a B. & O. R.R. "taxi"
#309	15¢	Raymond Ostrander Smith	1903	Henry Clay	From an engraving by A. Sealey
#327	10¢	C. Aubrey Huston	1904	Louisiana Purchase	From a U.S. Land Office map
#328	1¢	C. Aubrey Huston	1907	Captain John Smith	From a painting in the Virginia State Library
#329	2¢	C. Aubrey Huston	1907	Founding of Jamestown	From a painting
#330	5¢	C. Aubrey Huston	1907	Pocahontas	From an engraving in Capt. John Smith's *Generall Historie*
#367	2¢	C. Aubrey Huston	1909	Abraham Lincoln	From a statue by Augustus Saint-Gaudens
#370	2¢	C. Aubrey Huston	1909	William H. Seward	From a photograph
#372	2¢	Marcus W. Baldwin	1909	"Half Moon" & "Clermont"	From a drawing and photograph
#397	1¢	C. Aubrey Huston	1913	Vasco Núñez de Balboa	From an engraving
#400a	10¢	C. Aubrey Huston	1913	Discovery of San Francisco Bay	From a painting by Charles F. Mathews
#537	3¢	C. Aubrey Huston	1919	"Liberty Victorious" (Allied Victory)	From symbolic materials
#548	1¢	C. Aubrey Huston	1920	"Mayflower"	From a watercolor by Harrison Eastman
#549	2¢	C. Aubrey Huston	1920	Pilgrim Landing	From a bank note sketch by White
#551	1/2¢	C. Aubrey Huston	1925	Nathan Hale	From a Yale University statue by Bela Lyon Pratt
#552	1¢	C. Aubrey Huston	1923	Benjamin Franklin	From a bust by Jean Antoine Houdon
#555	3¢	C. Aubrey Huston	1923	Abraham Lincoln	From a photograph
#557	5¢	C. Aubrey Huston	1922	Theodore Roosevelt	From a photograph
#561	9¢	C. Aubrey Huston	1923	Thomas Jefferson	From a painting by Gilbert Stuart
#562	10¢	C. Aubrey Huston	1923	James Monroe	From a painting by John Vanderlyn
#565	14¢	C. Aubrey Huston	1923	Brule Sioux Chief Hollow Horn Bear	From a 1905 photograph by De Lancey Gill
#566	15¢	C. Aubrey Huston	1923	Statue of Liberty	From a photograph by Charles Skinner
#568	25¢	C. Aubrey Huston	1922	Niagara Falls	From a photograph by M. Handy Evans
#569	30¢	C. Aubrey Huston	1923	Bison	From a photograph by Charles R. Knight
#571	$1.00	C. Aubrey Huston	1923	Lincoln Memorial	From a photograph
#572	$2.00	C. Aubrey Huston	1923	U.S. Capitol	From a photograph
#615	2¢	C. Aubrey Huston	1924	Walloons landing at Albany NY	From an 1877 engraving
#617	1¢	C. Aubrey Huston	1925	Washington at Cambridge	From a "photoglyptic" chart
#618	2¢	C. Aubrey Huston	1925	Battle of Lexington	From a painting by Henry Sandham (based on a battle engraving by Amos Doolittle)
#619	5¢	C. Aubrey Huston	1925	Minute Man	From a statue by Daniel Chester French

Scott	Denomination	Designer	Issued	Subject	Source
#621	5¢	C. Aubrey Huston	1925	Viking Ship	From an 1893 World's Columbian Exposition photograph
#627	2¢	C. Aubrey Huston	1926	Liberty Bell	From a photograph (of a replica)
#628	5¢	C. Aubrey Huston	1926	John Ericsson Memorial	From a statue by James Earl Fraser
#629	2¢	C. Aubrey Huston	1926	Battle of White Plains	From a painting by Edmund F. Ward
#643	2¢	Alvin R. Meissner. C. Aubrey Huston	1927	Green Mountain Boy	From a drawing by the designers
#644	2¢	C. Aubrey Huston	1927	Burgoyne Surrender at Saratoga	From a painting by John Trumbull
#645	2¢	C. Aubrey Huston	1928	Washington at Prayer, Valley Forge	From a painting by Henry Brueckner
#649	2¢	C. Aubrey Hyston	1928	Wright Brothers Airplane	From photographs
#651	2¢	C. Aubrey Huston	1929	George Rogers Clark's capture of Fort Sackville	From a painting by Frederick C. Yohn
#654	2¢	Alvin R. Meissner	1929	Edison's First Lamp	From a drawing by the designer
#682	2¢	C. Aubrey Huston, Alvin R. Meissner	1930	Massachusetts Bay Colony	From the colonial seal
#683	2¢	A.R. Meissner, C. Aubrey Huston	1930	Charleston-Carolina 250th Anniversary	From a sketch by H.F. Church
#689	2¢	Alvin R. Meissner	1930	Baron Frederick von Steuben	From a medallion by Karl Dautert
#690	2c	Alvin R. Meissner	1931	General Casimir Pulaski	From an etching by H.B. Hall
#702	2¢	Alvin R. Meissner	1931	Red Cross	From a Red Cross poster
#703	2¢	C. Aubrey Huston	1931	Yorktown: Rochambeau/ Washington/ de Grasse	From Library of Congress engravings, and the John Trumbull painting
#704	1/2¢	C. Aubrey Huston	1932	George Washington	From a painting by Charles Willson Peale
#705	1¢	Alvin R. Meissner	1932	George Washington	From a bust by Jean Antoine Houdon
#706	1-1/2¢	C. Aubrey Huston	1932	George Washington	From a painting by Charles Willson Peale
#707	2¢	C. Aubrey Huston	1932	George Washington	From a painting by Gilbert Stuart
#708	3¢	C. Aubrey Huston	1932	George Washington	From a painting by Charles Willson Peale
#709	4¢	Alvin R. Meissner	1932	George Washington	From a painting by Charles Willson Peale
#710	5¢	Alvin R. Meissner	1932	George Washington	From a painting by Charles Willson Peale
#711	6¢	C. Aubrey Huston	1932	George Washington	From a painting by John Trumbull
#712	7¢	C. Aubrey Huston	1932	George Washington	From a painting by John Trumbull
#713	8¢	C. Aubrey Huston	1932	George Washington	From a drawing by Charles V. F. de St. Saint Memin
#714	9¢	C. Aubrey Huston	1932	George Washington	From a pastel by W. Williams
#715	10¢	Alvin R. Meissner	1932	George Washington	From a painting by Gilbert Stuart
#724	3¢	Victor S. McCloskey, Jr.	1932	William Penn	From a 1666 London painting
#725	3¢	C. Aubrey Huston	1932	Daniel Webster	From a bust by Daniel Chester French (completed by his daughter)
#726	3¢	C. Aubrey Huston	1933	General Oglethorpe	From an 18th century London painting
#727	3¢	Alvin R. Meissner	1933	Washington's Headquarters at Newburgh NY	From a painting by Robert W. Weir
#728	1¢	Victor S. McCloskey, Jr.	1933	Fort Dearborn	From a photograph of a replica
#732	3¢	Victor S. McCloskey, Jr.	1933	NRA (National Recovery Act)	From a painting by Henry Hintermeister
#733	3¢	Victor S. McCloskey, Jr.	1933	Byrd Antarctic Expedition II	From a sketch by Franklin D. Roosevelt
#734	5¢	Victor S. McCloskey, Jr.	1933	General Tadeusz Kosciuszko	From a statue by Anton Popiel
#736	3¢	Alvin R. Meissner	1934	The "Ark" and the "Dove"	From a poster by Edwin Tunis
#737	3¢	Victor S. McCloskey, Jr.	1934	Whistler's "Mother"	From the Louvre painting
#740	1¢	Victor S. McCloskey, Jr.	1934	El Capitan, Yosemite National Park CA	From a National Park Service photograph
#741	2¢	Victor S. McCloskey, Jr.	1934	Grand Canyon National Park AZ	From a National Park Service photograph
#742	3¢	Victor S. McCloskey, Jr.	1934	Mirror Lake, Mount Ranier National Park WA	From a National Park Service photograph
#744	5¢	Victor S. McCloskey, Jr.	1934	Old Faithful Geyser, Yellowstone National Park WY	From a photograph by J.E. Haynes
#745	6¢	Victor S. McCloskey, Jr.	1934	Wizard Island and Crater Lake, Crater Lake National Park OR	From a National Park Service photograph
#746	7¢	Victor S. McCloskey, Jr.	1934	Great Head, Acadia National Park ME	From a photograph by H.L. Bradley
#747	8¢	Victor S. McCloskey, Jr.	1934	Great White Throne, Zion National Park UT	From a photograph by George H. Grant
#748	9¢	Victor S. McCloskey, Jr.	1934	Mt. Rockwell, Glacier National Park MT	From a photograph by George H. Grant
#772	3¢	Victor S. McCloskey, Jr	1935	Connecticut Tercentennial "Charter Oak"	From a painting in the Connecticut State House
#774	3¢	Victor S. McCloskey, Jr.	1935	Boulder Dam	From a photograph
#776	3¢	Alvin R. Meissner	1936	Sam Houston/ The Alamo/ Stephen F. Austin	From drawings by S. Salamo and T. A. Butler, and a photo

Scott	Denomination	Designer	Issued	Subject	Source
#777	3¢	Alvin R. Meissner	1936	Roger Williams/ Rhode Island Tercentennial	From a statue in Providence RI
#783	3c	Alvin R. Meissner	1936	Oregon Territory Centennial	From U.S. government maps
#784	3c	Victor S. McCloskey, Jr.	1936	Susan B. Anthony	From a bust by Adelaide Johnson
#787	3¢	Victor S. McCloskey, Jr.	1937	W.T. Sherman/ U.S. Grant/ Philip Sheridan	From photographs by Brady; an engraving by H..L. Hatch
#788	4¢	William K. Schrage	1937	R.E. Lee/ home/Thomas J. "Stonewall" Jackson	From photographs by Vannerson, Rontzohn
#789	5¢	Capt. L.E. Schick	1937	U.S. Military Academy (West Point)	From a drawing by the designer
#790	1¢	Alvin R. Meissner	1936	Captains John Paul Jones/ John Barry	From an engraving, and a painting (by Gilbert Stuart)
#792	3¢	Alvin R. Meissner	1937	Captains David G. Farragut/ David D. Porter	From a photograph by Matthew Brady and a painting by Carl Becker
#794	5¢	Alvin R. Meissner	1937	US Naval Academy/Seal	From photographs at the Academy
#795	3¢	Alvin R. Meissner	1937	Northwest Territory Ordinance/ Manasseh Cutler/ Rufus Putnam	From an engraving by J.C. Buttre, and a painting by John Trumbull
#796	5¢	William A. Roach William K. Schrage	1937	Virginia Dare's family	From a drawing by William A. Roach
#798	3¢	Alvin R. Meissner	1937	Signing of the Constitution	From a painting by J.B. Stearns
#799	3¢	Alvin R. Meissner	1937	Hawaii	From a statue of King Kamehameha I, Honolulu
#800	3¢	Victor S. McCloskey, Jr.	1937	Alaska/ Mt. McKinley	From a Department of Interior photograph
#801	3¢	William K. Schrage, William A. Roach	1937	Puerto Rico/ La Fortaleza	From a photograph of the governor's palace
#802	3¢	Victor S. McCloskey, Jr.	1937	Virgin Islands/ Charlotte Amalie	From a photograph
#803	1/2¢	William K. Schrage	1938	Benjamin Franklin	From a statue by James Earl Fraser
#807	3¢	William K. Schrage	1938	Thomas Jefferson	From a bust by Jean Antoine Houdon
#816	11¢	Robert L. Miller, Jr.	1938	James K. Polk	From a U.S. Mint medallion
#836	3¢	Alvin R. Meissner	1938	Swedish/Finnish Colonists' Tercentennial	From a painting by Stanley M. Arthurs
#852	3¢	William A. Roach	1939	Golden Gate Exposition "Tower of the Sun"	From a photograph by Gabriel Maulin
#853	3¢	C. Dale Badgeley	1939	New York World's Fair Trylon & Perisphere	From the official Fair motif
#854	3¢	Alvin R. Meissner	1939	Sesquicentennial Inauguration of George Washington	From an 1859 engraving (with railing added)
#855	3¢	William A. Roach	1939	Baseball Centennial	From a drawing by the designer
#856	3¢	William A. Roach	1939	Roosevelt/Goethals/ Panama Canal 25th Anniversary	From photographs
#857	3¢	William K. Schrage	1939	300th Anniversary, Printing in America/ Stephen Daye Press	From a drawing by George F. Trenholm
#859	1¢	William A. Roach	1940	Washington Irving	From a Matthew Brady daguerreotype
#860	2¢	William A. Roach	1940	James Fenimore Cooper	From a Matthew Brady daguerreotype
#861	3¢	William A. Roach	1940	Ralph Waldo Emerson	From a photograph by Warren's Portraits
#862	5¢	William A. Roach	1940	Louisa May Alcott	From a photograph in *Demorest Family Magazine*
#863	10¢	William A. Roach	1940	Mark Twain	From a photograph by A. Claran
#864	1¢	William A. Roach	1940	Henry Wadsworth Longfellow	From a photograph by Sarony
#865	2¢	William A. Roach	1940	John Greenleaf Whittier	From a photograph by Warren's Portraits
#866	3¢	William A. Roach	1940	James Russell Lowell	From an 1855 drawing by S.W. Rowse
#867	5¢	William A. Roach	1940	Walt Whitman	From a Library of Congress photograph
#873	10¢	William A. Roach	1940	Booker T. Washington	From a 1909 photo by Harris & Ewing
#874	1¢	William A. Roach	1940	John James Audubon	From a Matthew Brady daguerreotype
#875	2¢	William A. Roach	1940	Crawford W. Long	From a Library of Congress engraving
#876	3¢	William A. Roach	1940	Luther Burbank	From a photograph
#879	1¢	William A. Roach	1940	Stephen Collins Foster	From a tintype
#880	2¢	William A. Roach	1940	John Philip Sousa	From a photograph
#881	3¢	William A. Roach	1940	Victor Herbert	From a photograph
#882	5¢	William A. Roach	1940	Edward A. MacDowell	From a *Musical America* photograph
#884	1¢	William A. Roach	1940	Gilbert Stuart	From a miniature by Sarah Goodrich
#885	2¢	William A. Roach	1940	James A. McNeill Whistler	From a photograph
#886	3¢	William A. Roach	1940	Augustus Saint-Gaudens	From a Washington Public Library photograph
#887	5¢	William A. Roach	1940	Daniel Chester French	From a photograph
#888	10¢	William A. Roach	1940	Frederic Remington	From a photograph

Scott	Denomination	Designer	Issued	Subject	Source
#889	1¢	William A. Roach	1940	Eli Whitney	From a painting by Alonzo Chappel
#890	2¢	William A. Roach	1940	Samuel F.B. Morse	From a photograph by Matthew Brady
#891	3¢	William A. Roach	1940	Cyrus Hall McCormick	From a painting by George P.A. Healy
#892	5¢	William A. Roach	1940	Elias Howe	From a Washington Public Library photograph
#893	10¢	William A. Roach	1940	Alexander Graham Bell	From a Library of Congress photograph
#894	3¢	William A. Roach	1940	Pony Express rider	From a drawing by the designer
#898	3¢	Victor S. McCloskey, Jr.	1940	Coronado Expedition	From a painting by Gerald Cassidy
#902	3¢	William A. Roach	1940	75th Anniversary, 13th Amendment	From a statue by Thomas Ball
#905	5¢	Mark O'Dea, William A. Roach	1942	Win the War	From a drawing by Harold Wescott
#909 to #920	5¢ ea	American Bank Note Company	1943	Overrun European countries: Poland, Czechoslovakia, Norway, Luxembourg, Netherlands, Belgium, France, Greece, Yugoslavia, Albania, Austria, Denmark	From a sketch by Franklin D. Roosevelt
#922	3¢	William A. Roach	1944	75th Anniversary, Transcontinental Railroad	From a mural by John McQuarrie
#925	3¢	William A. Roach	1944	Corregidor/Forts Drum, Frank, Hughes	From a newspaper sketch by Logan U. Reaves
#928	5¢	Victor S. McCloskey, Jr.	1945	United Nations Organizing Conference	---
#929	3¢	Victor S. McCloskey, Jr.	1945	Capture of Mount Suribachi, Iwo Jima	From a combat photograph by Joe Rosenthal
#933	5¢	William A. Roach, Victor S. McCloskey, Jr.	1946	FDR/Four Freedoms	From a 1935 photograph
#934	3¢	William A. Roach	1945	U.S. Army/ Arc de Triomphe	From a composite War Department photograph
#945	3¢	William K. Schrage	1947	Thomas A. Edison	From a 1919 photograph
#948	15¢	Robert L. Miller, Jr.	1947	Souvenir Sheet: US Postage Stamp Centennial	From original die proofs by Rawdon, Wright, Hatch, and Edson
#950	3¢	Charles R. Chickering	1947	Utah Centennial	From a drawing by the designer
#951	3¢	Andrew H. Hepburn	1947	"U.S.S. Constitution"	From original plans
#953	3¢	William A. Roach, Robert L. Miller, Jr.	1948	George Washington Carver	From a photograph
#959	3¢	Victor S. McCloskey, Jr.	1948	Stanton/Catt/Mott, Progress of Women Centennial	From photographs
#962	3¢	Victor S. McCloskey, Jr.	1948	Francis Scott Key, Key home/ Fort McHenry	From original drawings
#966	3¢	Victor S. McCloskey, Jr.	1948	Mt. Palomar Observatory	From a photograph
#967	3¢	Charles R. Chickering	1948	Clara Barton/ Red Cross	From a photograph
#975	3¢	Charles R. Chickering	1948	Will Rogers	From a Hollywood studio photograph
#976	3¢	Charles R. Chickering	1948	Fort Bliss Rocket	From composite drawings and photographs
#984	3¢	Charles R. Chickering	1949	Annapolis Tercentary	From a contemporary map and drawing
#986	3¢	William A. Roach, Robert L. Miller, Jr.	1949	Edgar Allan Poe	From an engraving by F.T. Stuart
#989	3¢	Victor S. McCloskey, Jr.	1950	"Freedom," Capitol dome	From the statue by Thomas Crawford
#990	3¢	William K. Schrage	1950	White House	From a Department of Interior photograph
#997	3¢	Victor S. McCloskey, Jr.	1950	California Statehood Centennial	From a drawing by Victor Berkowitz
#1003	3¢	Charles R. Chickering	1951	175th Anniversary: Battle of Brooklyn	From a painting by H.A. Ogden
#1004	3¢	Victor S. McCloskey, Jr.	1952	Betsy Ross Bicentennial	From a painting by C.H. Weisgerber
#1008	3¢	Charles R. Chickering	1952	3rd Anniversary, NATO	From a State Department photograph
#1010	3¢	Victor S. McCloskey, Jr.	1952	175th Anniversary: Lafayette's Arrival in America	From an engraving
#1011	3¢	William K. Schrage	1952	Mount Rushmore Memorial	From two photographs and a picture postcard
#1013	3¢	William K. Schrage, Robert L. Miller, Jr.	1952	Armed Services Women	From a Defense Department publicity photograph (of four Powers models)
#1017	3¢	Charles R. Chickering	1953	US National Guard	From a photograph
#1026	3¢	William K. Schrage	1953	General George S. Patton, Jr. / Armored Forces	From Defense Department materials
#1027	3¢	Charles R. Chickering	1953	New York City/ New Amsterdam Tercentennial	From a 17th century engraving
#1028	3¢	Charles R. Chickering	1953	Gadsden Purchase Centennial	From composite photographs
#1041	8¢	Charles R. Chickering	1954	Statue of Liberty	From a photograph
#1042A	8¢	R.J. Jones	1961	John J. Pershing	From a painting by J.F. Bouchor

Scott	Denomination	Designer	Issued	Subject	Source
#1048	25¢	Victor S. McCloskey, Jr., Charles R. Chickering	1958	Paul Revere	From a portrait by Gilbert Stuart
#1053	$5.00	C.R. Chickering, Victor S. McCloskey, Jr.	1956	Alexander Hamilton	From a painting by John Trumbull
#1061	3¢	Charles R. Chickering	1954	Kansas Territory Centennial	From a drawing by the designer
#1062	3¢	William K. Schrage	1954	George Eastman	From a 1921 photograph by Nahum E. Luboshez
#1063	3¢	Charles R. Chickering	1954	Lewis and Clark Expedition Sesquicentennial	From statues by Charles Keck and Leonard Crunelle
#1067	3¢	Charles R. Chickering	1955	Armed Forces Reserve	From a photograph
#1070	3¢	George R. Cox, Victor S. McCloskey, Jr.	1955	Atoms for Peace	From a drawing by George R. Cox
#1073	3¢	Charles R. Chickering	1956	Benjamin Franklin 250th Anniversary	From a painting by Benjamin West
#1074	3¢	Charles R. Chickering	1956	Booker T. Washington birthplace	From a photograph taken near Hale's Ford VA
#1077	3¢	Bob Hines, Victor S. McCloskey, Jr.	1956	Wild Turkey	From a drawing by Bob Hines
#1079	3¢	Bob Hines, Victor S. McCloskey, Jr.	1956	King Salmon Migration	From a drawing by Bob Hines
#1082	3¢	Victor S. McCloskey, Jr.	1956	Labor Day	From a mural by Lumen M. Winter
#1097	4¢	Victor S. McCloskey, Jr.	1957	Old Glory	From a sketch by the designer
#1098	3¢	Bob Hines, Charles R. Chickering	1957	Whooping Cranes	From a drawing by Bob Hines
#1099	3¢	Robert Geissmann	1957	Religious Freedom	From a drawing by the designer
#1107	3¢	Ervine Metzl, C.R. Chickering, William K. Schrage	1958	International Geophysical Year	From Michelangelo's fresco "The Creation of Adam," and a photograph of intense solar activity
#1113	1¢	Ervine Metzl, Charles R. Chickering	1959	Abraham Lincoln Sesquicentennial	From an 1860 painting by George P. A. Healy
#1115	4¢	Ervine Metzl, William K. Schrage	1958	Lincoln-Douglas Debates Centennial	From a drawing
#1120	4¢	William H. Buckley, C.R. Chickering, Sam Marsh	1958	Overland Mail Centennial	From a drawing by William H. Buckley
#1134	4¢	Robert Foster, Victor S. McCloskey, Jr.	1959	Petroleum Industry Centennial	From a drawing by Robert Foster
#1193	4¢	Charles R. Chickering	1962	Project Mercury Capsule	From a drawing by Charles de M. Barnes
#1198	4¢	Charles R. Chickering	1962	Homestead Act Centennial	From an 1890 photo of John Bakken's North Dakota sod hut
#1241	5¢	Robert L. Miller, Jr.	1963	Audubon's "Birds"	From a print in the National Gallery of Art
#1264	5¢	Richard Hurd, Sam Marsh	1965	Winston Churchill	From a photo by Yusuf Karsh
#1285	8¢	Frank Sebastiano	1966	Albert Einstein	From a photo by Philippe Halsman
#1286A	12¢	Norman Todhunter	1968	Henry Ford	From a portrait
#1287	13¢	Stevan Dohanos, R.J. Jones	1967	John F. Kennedy	From a photograph by Jacques Lowe
#1290	25¢	Walter DuBois Richards	1967	Frederick Douglass	From a photograph
#1292	40¢	Robert Geissmann, R.J. Jones	1968	Thomas Paine	From a portrait by John Wesley Jarvis
#1327	5¢	Leonard Baskin, R.J. Jones	1967	Henry David Thoreau	From the 1856 Maxham daguerreotype
#1354	6¢	R.J. Jones, L.E. Buckley, H.C. Mildner	1968	1775 Navy Jack	From the flag flown by Esek Hopkins in the Bahamas
#1371	6¢	Leonard Buckley	1969	Apollo 8 Moon Mission	From a NASA photograph
#1393	8¢	Robert Geissman, Leonard Buckley	1970	Dwight D. Eisenhower	From a photograph by George Tames
#1424	6¢	Paul Calle	1971	Douglas MacArthur	From a combat photograph
#1475	8¢	Robert Indiana	1973	"LOVE"	From a motif by the designer
#1499	8¢	Bradbury Thompson, V. Jack Ruther	1973	Harry S. Truman	From a photograph by Leo Stern
#1510	10¢	Dean Ellis, Ronald C. Sharpe	1973	Jefferson Memorial	From a photograph
#1529	10¢	Robert T. McCall, V. Jack Ruther	1974	Skylab IV in Earth Orbit	From NASA drawings and photographs
#1569	10¢	Robert T. McCall Ronald C. Sharpe	1975	Apollo/Soyuz after docking	From NASA drawings/photographs
#1771	13¢	Bernard Brussel-Smith, Peter Cocci	1977	Niagara River Peace Bridge	From a woodcut by Bernard Brussel-Smith, and a photograph
#1770	15¢	Bradbury Thompson	1979	Robert Fitzgerald Kennedy	From a photograph by Stanley Tretick
#1771	15¢	Jerry Pinkney	1979	Rev. Martin Luther King, Jr.	From drawings by the designer
#1773	15¢	Bradbury Thompson	1979	John Steinbeck	From a photograph by Philippe Halsman
#1889A	18¢ ea	James Brandenburg	1981	Bighorn Sheep, Puma, Harbor Seal, Bison, Brown Bear, Polar Bear, Wapiti, Moose, White-tailed Deer, Pronghorn Antelope	From photographs by the designer
#2046	20¢	Richard Gangel	1983	Babe Ruth	From a newspaper photograph
#2089	20¢	Richard Gangel	1984	Jim Thorpe	From a photograph
#2094	20¢	Bradbury Thompson	1984	Herman Melville	From a painting by J.O. Eaton

Scott	Denom-ination	Designer	Issued	Subject	Source
#2105	20¢	Bradbury Thompson	1984	Eleanor Roosevelt	From a photograph by A. David Gurewitsch, M.D.
#2109	20¢	Paul Calle	1984	Vietnam Memorial	Memorial designed by Maya Ying Lin
#2152	22¢	Richard Sheaff	1985	Korean Veterans	From a photograph by David Douglas Duncan
#2154	22¢	Richard Sheaff	1985	World War I Veterans	From a battlefield sketch by Capt. Harvey Dunn
#2178	15¢	Jack Rosenthal	1988	"Buffalo Bill" Cody	From a dining car menu photograph
#2183	25¢	Richard Sparks	1986	Jack London	From a photograph by Charmian London
#C3	24¢	C. Aubrey Huston	1918	Curtiss "Jenny"	From a photograph
#C3a	24¢	C. Aubrey Huston	1918	(inverted "Jenny")	From a photograph
#C9	20¢	C. Aubrey Huston	1926	Mail Planes over US Map	From a drawing by the designer
#C11	5¢	Alvin R. Meissner	1928	Rocky Mountain aerial beacon, Sherman Hill	From a photograph
#C23	6¢	William K. Schrage	1938	Bald Eagle	From the Library of Congress bookplate
#C45	6¢	Charles R. Chickering	1949	Wright Brothers and "Flyer A"	From a drawing and Smithsonian photographs
#C48	4¢	Edward R. Grove	1954	Bald Eagle	From a drawing by Edwin R. Grove

Scott	Denom-ination	Designer	Issued	Subject	Source
#C76	10¢	Paul Calle	1969	Moon Landing	From a painting by Paul Calle based on NASA photographs
#Q1	1¢	C. Aubrey Huston	1912	Post Office Clerk	From a photograph
#Q5	5¢	C. Aubrey Huston	1912	Mail Train	From a photograph
#Q6	10¢	C. Aubrey Huston	1912	Steamship and Mail Tender	From a photograph
#Q7	15¢	C. Aubrey Huston	1912	Automobile Mail Delivery	From a photograph
#Q8	20¢	C. Aubrey Huston	1912	Airplane Mail Delivery	From a photograph
#Q9	25¢	C. Aubrey Huston	1912	Factory	From a photograph
#U348	1¢	Bureau of Engraving and Printing	1893	Columbus/Liberty Envelope	---

CONFEDERATE STATES

Scott	Denom-ination	Designer	Issued	Subject	Source
#11	10¢	F. Joubert. Printed by de la Rue & Co., London, England	1862	Jefferson Davis	From a photograph

GUAM

Scott	Denom-ination	Designer	Issued	Subject	Source
#2	2¢	Bureau of Engraving and printing (over-printed U.S. #248)	1899	George Washington	From a bust by Jean Antoine Houdon

PHILIPPINES

Scott	Denom-ination	Designer	Issued	Subject	Source
#215	3¢	Bureau of Engraving and printing (over-printed U.S. #253)	1899	Andrew Jackson	From a statue by Hiram Powers

INDEX

The text and display types in this book were set
in a digitized version of Goudy Old Style,
a typeface created by the famous American type designer
Frederic William Goudy (1865-1947).
Goudy's prolific typographic output was exceeded only by
the legendary Giambattista Bodoni (1740-1813).
Between 1911 and 1922 alone,
Goudy completed sixty-seven typeface designs
and produced at least two dozen American types,
of which this face is one of the most popular.

❧

Computerized page composition by
THE DESIGN OFFICE, INC.
New York City.

Printed on
WARREN 80 lb. LUSTRO GLOSS OFFSET ENAMEL
and bound in
HOLLISTON ARRESTOX A
by
ARCATA GRAPHICS COMPANY
Kingsport TN

Typography by
JOSEPH FEIGENBAUM

Computer typesetting by
ELIZABETH CASTAGNA

Macrophotography by
TOM FITZGERALD

❧

Design by
CHARLES DAVIDSON

"Neither snow nor rain nor heat nor
gloom of night stays these couriers from the swift
completion of their appointed rounds."
--HERODOTUS